C A P S T O N E

✔ KU-585-606

INSTANT · KNOWLEDGE

Smart

THINGS TO KNOW ABOUT

Consultancy

PATRICK FORSYTH

First published 2002 by
Capstone Publishing Ltd (A John Wiley & Sons Co.)
8 Newtec Place
Magdalen Road
Oxford OX4 1RE
United Kingdom
http://www.capstoneideas.com

British Library Cataloguing in Publication Data
A CIP catalogue record for this book is available from the British Library

ISBN 1-84112-438-9

Typeset by
Forewords, 109 Oxford Road, Cowley, Oxford
Printed and bound by
T.J. International Ltd, Padstow, Cornwall

This book is printed on acid-free paper

Contents

What is Smart?

The *Smart* series is a new way of learning. *Smart* books will improve your understanding and performance in some of the critical areas you face to-day like *customers, strategy, change, e-commerce, brands, influencing skills, knowledge management, finance, teamworking, partnerships.*

Smart books summarize accumulated wisdom as well as providing original cutting-edge ideas and tools that will take you out of theory and into action.

The widely respected business guru Chris Argyris points out that even the most intelligent individuals can become ineffective in organizations. Why? Because we are so busy working that we fail to learn about ourselves. We stop reflecting on the changes around us. We get sucked into the patterns of behavior that have produced success for us in the past, not realizing that it may no longer be appropriate for us in the fast-approaching future.

There are *three* ways the Smart series helps prevent this happening to you:

- by increasing your self-awareness

- by developing your understanding, attitude and behavior

- by giving you the tools to challenge the status quo that exists in your organization.

Smart people need smart organizations. You could spend a third of your career hopping around in search of the Holy Grail, or you could begin to create your own smart organization around you today.

Finally a reminder that books don't change the world, people do. And although the *Smart* series offers you the brightest wisdom from the best practitioners and thinkers, these books throw the responsibility on you to apply what you're learning in your work.

Because the truly smart person knows that reading a book is the start of the process and not the end . . .

As Eric Hoffer says, 'In times of change, learners inherit the world, while the learned remain beautifully equipped to deal with a world that no longer exists.'

David Firth
Smartmaster

Acknowledgements

I have only been able to write this book because of
the time I have myself spent working as a consultant,
first in a medium-sized consulting firm and then with
my own firm, which I started in partnership with a
colleague in 1990. My background is in marketing
and this has been a main focus for much of my work.
Training and development in its various forms has
also been a theme (I conduct public seminars,
in-house training courses and conferences and
one-to-one tutorials, as well as creating training materials), as well as
conventional consultancy, research and other advisory work.

> SMART QUOTES
>
> Good advice is
> beyond price
>
> Latin proverb

Furthermore, I have only been able to work as I have because of the
experience gained over the years in a process where many other people
have acted as catalysts. So thanks are due to many of those with whom I
have worked for the knowledge they passed on so generously and the
time they took to help me develop and refine my own skills. Without
meaning to exclude others, perhaps I could mention particularly first

Mike Wilson. He brought me into the consulting world, and ran a company in which it was both possible to learn fast and where, though facing new challenges was the norm, the culture of mutual support made it possible to succeed. And secondly, David Senton, with whom I have worked closely throughout my career and who offered specific assistance with this book.

The material that follows draws a little on an earlier book *Marketing Professional Services;* and my work with a variety of other consultancy firms in that sector has also helped. Like this one, that earlier book was commissioned by Mark Allin, now of Capstone Publishing. He is both a great innovator in the business publishing world and the kind of editor with which any author would be pleased to work; I owe him thanks with regard to a number of projects. Similar sentiments apply to his colleague John Moseley with whom I have seen this particular book through. Thanks are due too to a number of friends, associates and contacts working in a variety of consulting roles whose ears I bent in writing this, and in some cases whose words I have quoted (if so, their names appear in context throughout the text).

Last – but definitely not least – thanks are due to those who have bought my own consultancy services over the years; without you goodness knows what I might have done.

Preface

You are an expert. Not just someone who can offer sensible advice, but someone who people would be willing to pay money to be advised by (or you would not be looking at this book). If we take that as read, certain questions remain. Do you want to earn your living this way? Would you enjoy working as a consultant? And, not least, could you make a success of it?

This book reviews these questions and more; it is designed to help you make up your mind and work in a way – before, during and after the consulting process – that makes it work and makes it pay. It takes a broad view of the description 'consultant'. Perhaps the main target reader is best summed up by the term management consultant, but that covers a multitude of sins and the book is intended to be relevant more broadly still. So, consultant here is used in the sense of someone who:

• Sells their expertise, and their time, for fees.

- Provides a service designed to assist a client or client organization improve or change things.

- Advises and, on occasion, gets involved in the implementation of the action inherent in that advice.

It is a description that includes some with an overall brief, to improve the overall organizational strategy. Others have a functional focus, working in production, say, or marketing only. Some are technical in a variety of ways ranging from chemical engineering consultants to designers. For others, specialist is a better word and there are those who operate in areas of company start-up, recruitment and selection (or conversely as what are euphemistically called outplacement consultants), change or management development and training – one of the areas of my own work. Another category of consultant falls under the heading of professional services. These include accountants, architects and lawyers who need to obtain professional qualifications. Every area of business has its consultants: these include computers and IT, market research, design, brand development, public relations – right through to some oddball ones; for instance, I once worked for someone who was a feng shui consultant to industrial clients.

If any of these is you, this book is designed to help you. If your particular take on consultancy is not listed here, no matter; if you aim to use your expertise to help others, then you should find the book useful.

In one sense any consultant is just an external supplier like any other, in another way they may be closely involved with the management team of their client (and sometimes – as with interim management – more permanently involved for a while at least). However they operate, indeed however their clients want them to operate, they have to be able to do so successfully.

If you are to work freelance, or set up a small consultancy practice, then the buck stops with you. There is more to be done than simply the work; however good you are at that, you must manage your finances, act to create some visibility for yourself and to obtain sufficient work, and keep up to date so that you can continue to operate effectively. You need to be a jack of all trades and, necessarily, master of many.

Not everyone whose mind is crossed by the thought *I'll be a consultant* goes on to become one, and only some amongst those who do both like it and make a go of it. However, if it suits you – and this book may help you take a view of that – it can be a most rewarding way to work; rewarding both financially and in terms of the work satisfaction it gives. If you want a completely biased view – it is a great career choice. No apologies for the bias, the book is positively intended to reflect my enthusiasm for consultancy. It offers how-to guidance, but that would be sterile without enthusiasm.

The subject of your consultancy, actual or planned, may be amongst a wide range of different kinds of consultancy, but the business process each involves is similar.

Patrick Forsyth
Touchstone Training & Consultancy
28 Saltcote Maltings
Maldon
Essex CM9 4QP
United Kingdom
Autumn 2002

1

Introduction: The Nature of Consultancy

What do consultants do? Consultants work in many different fields, but they all do, well, consultancy work – so far, so unhelpful. Like the range of areas in which a consultant may work, outlined in the Preface, the possibilities are wide. Consultancy work may involve:

- A duration of involvement varying from a few hours one-to-one mentoring to projects lasting many months.

- Work conducted on a solo basis or in association with others: this, in turn, might range from a team of consultants or a team involving consultants and members of the client organization's own staff, or a variety of other mixes.

- Exclusively advisory work (though based on investigation or research), or work that involves hands-on assistance with implementation.

- Projects conducted primarily on client's premises or elsewhere.

- Work in different geographical locations and environments – for example, overseas.

- Responding to a very specific brief or, at the other end of this range, effectively inventing the brief as the project proceeds.

- Objectives that may be designed to improve the information base, knowledge or skill of clients, or promote change in a variety of forms.

- Dealing with matters that clients are effectively unable to do (as the guy who sorts out my computer matters does) or do not want to do (recommending that staff levels be reduced).

Projects, whether large or small, may be charged for on a fixed project basis (which doubtless should reflect time taken), on a time basis – per hour, per day or whatever – or in other ways, even including payment by results.

SMART QUOTES

Management consultancy is an advisory service contracted for and provided to organizations by specially trained and qualified persons who assist, in an objective and independent manner, the client organization to identify problems, analyse these problems, recommend solutions to these problems, and help, when requested in the implementation of solutions.

L. Greiner and R. Metzger, *Consulting to Management*

The variety is clearly extensive. Indeed, one individual consultant may work in a variety of different ways.

An important resource

There is, let us be honest, a certain amount of cynicism about consultancy, and there is no lack of maxims and sayings to support this view.

> I come from an environment where, if you see a snake, you kill it. At General Motors, if you see a snake, the first thing you do is hire a consultant on snakes.
>
> Ross Perot, businessman and politician (then a Director of General Motors)

SMART QUOTES

On the other hand, legions of consultants exist and thrive and only do so because clients are satisfied with how they perform and what they achieve. Consultants are essentially like any external resource. When something must be done they provide one way of getting it done. Training, one of the areas in which I work, is a good example. Consider a simple requirement. It is identified within an organization that certain people require their skills extended in a particular area, maybe in making effective presentations. Simple action – just giving them a book about it, say – might be rejected as insufficient to the task; it is decided that a course is needed. This might be conducted internally, by a training manager, or a line manager, either already able to do this or prepared to take time to put themselves in a position to do so. Or it might be thought more cost and time effective to get a suitably experienced consultant to take on the job. The broad and specialist experience then brought to bear influences the decision.

SMART QUOTES

A consultant is someone who borrows your watch to tell you the time, and then keeps the watch.

Anon

The point is that in many projects, consultants do not represent the only way of tackling the job or achieving the desired results. If consultants, or some of them at least, did not do a good job, then they would not be hired, indeed would not exist.

Consultancy is big business. A very great deal of consultancy of all kinds is bought every year, a situation that exists across most industries and most countries (in countries where such services cannot be afforded, then much may be funded by government or international agencies).

The market is growing too, so if you are wondering if there is a market for your services, then at least in overall terms the answer is: yes. What is more, consultancy looks like it will continue to grow, a growth that is fuelled by the dynamic environment that seems likely to continue. Such factors as technological change, competitive pressures, international developments, legislation, environmental and ethical concerns, and the developing style and process of management all support this view.

Whatever amounts of work may be available to you, obtaining it and doing it involves a series of stages; all of these have to be well executed for the overall process to work.

The process of consultancy

The following series of stages form a cycle of activity. Because each stage is dependent on the others, success is only possible if you are able to execute every stage well.

KILLER QUESTIONS

How exactly does the business of consultancy work?

1. Marketing activity

2. Initial contact

3. Initial meeting

4. Situation analysis

5. Making proposals

6. Response and fine-tuning the brief

7. Agreement to proceed

8. Handling the project

9. On-going communications

10. Extending or varying the project

11. Conclusion

12. Continuing contact

Stage 12 is designed to link back, and complete the cycle. It forms a tangible part of marketing activity (one that recognizes that it is always easier to sell more to a satisfied client than to find a new one) and is designed to produce further business.

These stages are now commented on individually and in turn.

1. Marketing activity

However excellent and desirable your skills, you cannot expect business simply to walk in the door. Marketing activity is a necessity. There is a variety of marketing techniques to be deployed and the trick, especially on a small scale, is to use the techniques best suited to consultancy and its clients, and to use them well. What is required here is to create and maintain a continuum of marketing activity that will act to generate business, and to do so cost effectively.

A warning: consultants talk about 'feast and famine'. This describes the situation where, busy with work, little marketing gets done, then, as projects conclude, frantic (and sometimes less than ideal) efforts are made to fill the coming gap.

SMART QUOTES

> They say if you build a better mousetrap than your neighbour, people are going to come running. They are, like hell! It's marketing that makes the difference.
>
> Ed Johnson

2. Initial contact

Contacts made as a result of marketing activity must be well handled. Whether the person contacting you has responded to a mailshot, or just come across you in a directory or at a conference, their first contact is vital. They may know little about you initially and will read a good deal into the seemingly small signs visible at this stage.

So, not only must your first response be professional and persuasive, but every aspect of the process, from what you, or someone else, says when you answer the telephone to how messages are handled and how promptly an email message gets a reply, must be too. This stage may be personal, or may include other actions such as sending someone a brochure ahead of speaking to them again or meeting them face to face.

3. Initial meeting

This is a crucial stage. Few clients will hire you without meeting you, so the face-to-face meeting is an important part of the sales process. For you this is a sales meeting; for the prospective client it is an opportunity for evaluation. Much of the meeting is concerned with stage 4, below.

4. Situation analysis

Clients may be looking for someone to help in a number of ways. They may have a problem that needs solving. They may want help to take advantage of an opportunity.

Whatever their need, it must be clearly specified and agreed. Curiously perhaps, there are often occasions when clients are not actually very clear about what they want, or when their thoughts are (perhaps only because of lack of experience) not very logical or practical. Whatever the circumstances, a clear brief is essential before specific proposals can be made.

Your skill in helping people to define a brief is a valuable early demonstration of your professional competence. After all, is anyone who cannot get the brief straight promptly and easily likely to be hired to do anything?

5. Making proposals

Sometimes, most often with people you have worked with before, little formal documentation is necessary. Certainly many quite sophisticated projects are set up with little more than an exchange of emails and are none the worse for that. More often, however, proposals need to be formalized and they need to be in writing.

Your written proposal will say a good deal about you as well as setting out something about the brief and your recommendations for dealing with it.

It may also link to a presentation – the pitch or beauty parade as it is called in some fields of work – with the two together working to carry things forward; or not.

6. Refining and fine-tuning the brief

Sometimes the proposal document, and perhaps the associated presentation if there is one, prompts no further discussion. It may be followed simply by a yes or no. Sometimes it does prompt further thought or discussion – further meetings – or was designed as the first stage of a process where fine-tuning was recognized by both parties to be necessary.

It is a mistake to ignore the possibility of this stage and, when it occurs, it is one that can be valuable for both consultant and client – and ultimately for the project that may be agreed. For the consultant this is true in terms of both selling and defining the project and ensuring that it will go well.

7. Agreement to proceed

Once the client says yes, your first instinct may be to throw your hat in the air or pour yourself a celebratory drink; and why not? But there are other things to be done.

The first is to make sure that everything about what will now be done is clear and in writing, and the second is to consider any contractual aspects of the arrangement. Care at this stage can avoid awkward problems later.

8. Handling the project

Now, finally, you are at the stage of actually doing the work. This may be the core of the matter, but it is also, as we are seeing, still a part of the overall sales process.

9. Ongoing communication

Although communication is inherent to the consulting process, this is sufficiently important to be considered as a discrete stage. Whatever the nature of the work, clients want to be kept informed as to how it is going. This should have been specified in your proposals and must suit the client. Too much detail or too great a frequency of contact, and they worry about the time you are taking to do it; time they are paying for no doubt. Too little and they feel neglected or begin to doubt the soundness of the project.

Care is needed here in terms of both communications method and content. The longer the duration of the project then the more separate communications are likely to be needed along the way, and the greater the variety of methods (ranging from emails to meetings) they are likely to need to make them work.

10. Extending or varying the project

This too, although not always something that happens, is worth viewing as a stage in its own right. Sometimes, for good reasons or bad, projects change in progress. This needs agreeing and documenting. It may be the source of extra work for the consultant, of a better result for the client; or, at worst, of a falling out if what is done ends up not matching what the client felt was the agreed brief.

10. Conclusion

When a project has ended, something normally marks the fact. A final report is submitted, a final letter written or meeting held. For the client this is where they should feel a good decision was made – by them – that value for money has been received, and that results justify the project (even at a stage when more implementation remains to be done).

For you it can be the first stage in procuring follow-up work.

There is another important matter to be dealt with here. Although in longer projects there may well have been stage payments, you need to send them the (final) invoice; and, realistically, you may need further contact before it actually gets paid.

12. Continuing contact

Your likelihood of getting further or repeat work can be measured in direct proportion to the client's memory of you. Never assume that you did such a good job that they will remember you forever and think of no one else, especially alongside the likelihood of others being in touch with them. People are busy and consultants are many – you need to actively keep their memory of you fresh.

How you judge the frequency, method and content of messages you now send will condition things here. Well executed, such actions can produce more work and keep promotion and sales costs down.

An additional point here: be persistent. Maybe a client offers no great hope of immediate further work, but enquiries or work received two or three years on is still worth having. The cost of maybe ten contacts, some of which could be as simple as an email, over say three years is negligible in terms of time and cost if it produces more work. Certainly it is likely to compare favourably with the cost of finding another new client instead if contact is lost.

What you want is a regular flow of work. Sometimes what you have 'on the go' at a particular time will be a complete mixture in terms of the original point of contact. I began writing this three months after the possibility of my writing the book was first discussed. I have other current projects where the first action that led to them was not so long ago or much longer.

What makes a consultant

In light of what has been said above about the characteristics and competencies needed in a good consultant, you may already have a view. Of course, it does demand a bank of knowledge,

KILLER QUESTIONS

Is consultancy for you?

experience and competence in your chosen area of expertise. Here we will assume you have such and consider other matters.

Like anything else you might do, there are certain skills that are essential to success as a consultant. These are not all inherent, however. For example, consultancy demands good communications skills and it is perhaps unlikely that you will make a good consultant if you struggle with this in every way. There may, however, be something you can do about more minor shortfalls. Maybe your report-writing skills leave something to be desired. You can learn to improve them. It may take a little time, you may have to resolve to shed some bad habits, and it may need some study, consultation and practice – but it can be done. So, do not reject the idea because of one shortfall.

Q: How do I know if I am well suited to consultancy?

A: It may be worth undertaking a clear, objective analysis of yourself to see just how you do stack up and whether there are any specific areas where beefing up your skills would put you in a better position from which to succeed. This could perhaps be your first consultative project.

In other ways it is something to think seriously about. You could opt to join an existing consulting firm as a first step, doing so even if you plan to work independently later. In this case you need to deploy normal, or exceptional, job-seeking skills, though review of these is beyond our brief here.

Assuming you want to go it alone, it is worth considering certain questions:

- *Will the project nature of consulting work suit you?* I have never found this a problem, but have come across other people for whom the frustration they find in not seeing things right through cannot be tolerated, or who find that the process of working on a number of different projects in parallel is not a comfortable one.

- *How highly do you rate control?* As an independent, everything that happens is down to you. Everything. Some people like that; others miss the support.

- *Do you have the skills not only to do the work, but the broader skills needed to manage, market and sell your own business?* The ability to do all this – particularly to sell and do in parallel – is a prerequisite of success.

- *Are you self-sufficient and able to work alone?* There are things you can do to compensate, not least some systematic networking (discussed later), but some aspects of it can be a lonely business.

- *Do you have the discipline to work alone?* It may seem a detail, but there is no one else to see to it that you sit down at your desk at an appropriate time in the morning, or that if something is to catch today's post it is *you* who must go to the post box.

- *What about financial security and risk?* An independent consultant can earn a good living, and some do very well; but no work = no fees – if you have been used to the (comparative) security of a monthly salary coming in, going independent can be something of a shock to the system. This applies at the beginning (I remember having to write out a cheque to buy a car after twenty years of driving company ones, for example), and also on an ongoing basis.

- *Will it fit with your lifestyle?* Does the location in which you live make sense? How much travel is likely to be necessary? (And time away from home?) What hours will it be necessary to work and when? And more no doubt; if you have a partner what will their feelings be about it and, perhaps, how can they help or support you?

The above list does capture some of the key questions, but it cannot hope to be definitive. You need to think about your own situation, extend such a list and think about and answer the questions honestly. There are other criteria that you should think about as well.

The ideal consultant

The ideal consultant probably does not exist, and certainly the range of work that consultants do demands very different characteristics. Some of the special factors needed in specific kinds of work may be things you love or hate, are good at or not. For instance, early in my career I did just a little executive selections work, I prompted some good appointments too and that was satisfying, but I must confess that I found the seemingly endless interviewing ultimately tedious.

Some things are common, however, and you certainly should consider such factors as:

KILLER QUESTIONS

What factors are essential to being a good consultant?

- *Problem solving:* much consulting work will involve you in this. Problems may equate with difficulty in the negative sense, but they are as likely to be positive, concerned with puzzling out how to exploit an opportunity within the client organization. This is a process you must be able to do justice too

- *Analysis.* This goes hand in hand with problem solving. Consultants need an analytical turn of mind (one that in turn often, though not always, goes with being suitably numerate)

- *Creativity.* The solutions that you suggest following problem solving and analysis may well need some creativity. This is a difficult thing to define, but can be a crucial part of what consultants must deliver

- *Focus.* Another essential skill is focus, simplistically being good at seeing the wood as well as the trees. This may mean the ability to spot basic things that are perhaps being overlooked; it also implies being able to stand back and see the full picture.

The four factors above hang closely together; other, rather different factors should be mentioned as well:

- *Good organization.* You need to be well organized in the running of your own business and you also need to be – and appear – well organized in the conduct of consulting assignments. Good project management may be an inherent part of what is needed here

- *Enthusiasm.* Whatever you think of your clients and the work they want done (and sometimes it may be tedious or obvious – *What's the matter with these people?*) you must project, and therefore feel, some enthusiasm for it for your involvement to be acceptable. There may also be a need to enthuse people within a client organization in order to get their co-operation or participation; this is more necessary in some kinds of work than others (my training work is a good example)

- *Common sense* – which, it is often said, is not so common. Your client may be missing the obvious and over-engineering things, but you must have your feet firmly on the ground. Do not, on the other hand be arrogant

- *Communications.* Any consultant needs good communications skills. In particularly, a consultant needs to be able to write well, especially proposals and reports, in order to make effective presentations and perform well (and chair well) in meetings. Good communication – timely, clear and well pitched to its task – not only helps assignments along, it is also appreciated by clients. Bad communication can literally sink a consulting business

- *Authority.* This goes with the heading above. You need not only to be able to communicate clearly, but with some clout; on occasion with considerable clout. Not only that, but you must often be able to deliver it at senior level and hold your own. All the expertise in the world can be ineffective without this, though perhaps it should be added that this does not imply raw assertiveness or outright aggression; a suitable professional manner is necessary.

You need also to think of any special factors made necessary by the field in which you aim to work and personalize such a list in considering how well you meet the criteria. For example, what computer skills do you need? Probably you were well on your way to a decision here or this book would be of no interest, so, assuming it is for you, what comes next?

Setting up

What needs to be done to get you started? Many of the considerations are those that any new business must face. Here we focus on certain issues that are key to consultancy; if you need more guidance then there may be topics you need to research separately to get the detail. One such is planning.

You need a business plan. The formality of this may be dictated by external factors. For instance, if you want to raise money, then banks will insist on one. But, from your point of view, the thinking that goes into a plan is essential, and there is too much to think about, and too much at stake, to believe you have all the necessary details in your head. You need a written plan.

SMART VOICES

Not a business voice, but the key principle of business planning is elegantly illustrated by Lewis Carroll in *Alice's Adventures in Wonderland*:

'Would you tell me, please, which way I ought to go from here?'
'That depends a good deal on where you want to get to,' said the Cat.
'I don't much care where – ' said Alice.
'Then it doesn't matter which way you go,' said the Cat.
'– so long as get somewhere,' Alice added as an explanation.
'Oh, you're sure to do that,' said the Cat, 'if only you walk long enough.'

Elegantly and memorably put, and the Cheshire Cat's logic is surely very clear. Planning is essential as a basis for a well-run business; you need to plan and do so effectively – it enhances the likelihood of achieving what you want.

SMART QUOTES

A business plan – defined

A detailed plan setting out objectives of a business over a stated period, often three, five, or ten years. A business plan is drawn up by many businesses, especially if the business has passed through a bad period or if it has had a major change of policy. For new businesses it is an essential document for raising capital or loans. The plan should quantify as many of the objectives as possible, providing monthly cash flows and production figures for at least the first two years, with diminishing detail in subsequent years; it must also outline its strategy and the tactics it intends to use in achieving its objectives. Anticipated profit and loss accounts should form part of the business plan on a quarterly basis for at least two years, and an annual basis thereafter. For a group of companies the business plan is often called a corporate plan. (*Oxford Dictionary of Business*)

SMART VOICES

Business planning – a summary

Planning must be undertaken to provide a solid base from which the business can operate. It is, or should be, essentially practical. That is, doing the planning, and having the plan, should make it easier to run the business. Certainly it is sufficiently important that no new business, or new business development, is likely to be supported by an organization's bank without a sensible and well-documented plan being on the table. That alone is enough to make many people who doubt the value of business planning to think again.

The plan for the year – the annual plan - may well be an integral part of longer-term planning (say for three years ahead) with the operational plan for the immediate future linking to outline plans, and lines of thought, for the longer term. However it is defined in a particular organisation, a good plan will:

- Identify opportunities for future profit improvement
- Have the ability to anticipate dynamic external changes
- Provide better protection for the future of the business

- Prompt the collection of relevant data
- Allocate the company's resources towards specific ends
- Underpin the process of control
- Assist with clear communications around the company
- Focus individual efforts and assist personal motivation
- Provide a proper commercial reference for all activities
- Justify development (and development funds)

Further, if it is to be a practical process, it will help if:

- The approach is an integration of 'bottom up/top down' (i.e. it involves people throughout the company even if there are only two of you!).
- The system and purpose is clear to all.
- Standard (tailored) planning formats are used;
- A planning cycle, specifying all timings, is agreed.
- The planning includes a facility to 'fine-tune' (particularly to take advantage of opportunities).
- An eye is kept on the external reactions to everything done to facilitate 'fine-tuning'.

Some discipline may be required here as other pressures too easily intrude. In the context of this work and with smaller businesses in mind, while all aspects of business planning are important, the promotional aspects – the things that will bring in the business – are key. So often organizations refer to their business plan, and also to a marketing plan; the latter is simply a core element of the whole. That said, every aspect of the business needs planning.

Essentially you must ensure that you get planning to address issues that are important to you and your business, whatever they are and whatever their scale.

Adapted from the Capstone ExpressExec series title *Business Planning*.

The most important aspect of your plan is to help direct your business, for example focusing you on particular industries and markets, even particular job functions. Quite a few management consultants list preparing business plans for their clients among their offerings; if this includes you, then your own should be exemplary!

Other matters to be considered include:

The company vehicle you use

There are a number of options here (and the details will vary in different countries). For example, two main options in the United Kingdom are a limited company or a partnership (one half of which may not be [much] involved in the business). The criteria for decision here are legal and financial, and while you may – will – always have to pay tax, the kind of business enterprise you form will affect when and how you pay, and possibly how much. Simplistically, a partnership is easier to set up and administer, a limited company is more complex and expensive, but offers more protection in case of problems. Some work perfectly well as the sole proprietor of their own solo business.

Where you will work from

The first decision is geographic. Can you work in the field you choose from where you currently live? You need to consider where your clients are likely to be and the accessibility that exists twixt you and them. Do you need to be within easy (cheap, fast) reach of some main centre, for instance?

The next question is: do you need an office or can you work from home. Home working is now common, and there is really no real problem if people recognize that your address is a house rather than an office. However, if people are going to visit you, rather than your going to them, or if you are going to work with other people or need space for equipment or something, then you may need an office.

There are considerable differences with regard to both costs (obviously an office will increase your fixed costs) and the way in which you work. Some people thrive on working at home, others find that the interface between home and work (and children and family life) is very complicated, allowing justice to be done to neither. Think carefully. Home may be the best starting point for many people, though your plans may make it clear that an office is essential in due course. Most people agree that home working only really works if you have a dedicated area, preferably a room, and are not trying to work of the kitchen table with the food mixer buzzing in the background and the cat on your knee.

The name you trade under

You may well be stuck with this for some time, and changing names can present difficulties (and incur costs). The main intention here should be to pick something that will put across the right information and image and which will work for clients. We return to this in Chapter 4.

The other people with whom you will work

If other people are going to be important to the way you operate, then you need to have relationships in place early on. For example, you will need an accountant and it may be sensible to have one in place ahead of starting rather than only thinking of this at the end of your first year's trading. You may have a variety of other people you need to contact. Most freelance consultants have a network of 'brains to pick' on technical and other matters. You may also need ready access to other consultants who can work with you as subcontractors. Other people to have in mind might include those providing computer advice and back up, and printing or secretarial/administrative support. And maybe a

A suitable accountant

You will have enough to do finding and undertaking consulting work; you do not want to be worrying about whether you are entering the VAT correctly or mis-judge what tax provision you should make.

Beware: getting in a muddle in this area can prove very time-consuming and expensive.

financial advisor (do not, for instance, neglect your pension arrange-ments) and – if you can find one – a bank manager.

The resources you will need

Assuming that you are working alone to start with you will not need a vast array of resources and equipment, but you do need to think about it and get it right. A computer is, these days, essential to all. You may also want to have a back up. What happens if your computer is down and you cannot type a letter or access your e-mail. What else? Well, I still find my fax useful, I have a binding machine (for reports and proposals), and a mobile telephone seems simply ubiquitous. Add the plethora of bits and pieces of any office – paper, pens, paperclips and, hopefully, an in-tray – and you are up and running.

Beyond that, further equipment will reflect the work you do, a surveyor will need a drawing board and so on.

So far, so good, you have the skills, you want to move ahead and you have the main set up factors in mind. Before you can really make a start you need to consider one further major area in some detail: exactly what services will you offer? It is obviously necessary that you be clear about this before you can describe them to other people. It is to this we turn in the next chapter.

2

Deciding the Service Range

Any consultant must decide exactly what it is that they are going to do for their clients. If your expertise is in a particular area, then that is where you will want the focus of your business to be. As in any business you must, however, be sure that there is actually a market for this. If you plan to train people to juggle with flaming torches, then, provided you have the skill (and fireproof carpets), you may well be able to do an excellent job. But how many people will beat a path to your door? More seriously, you are probably contemplating something more routine, you know that there is a market for it and that other consultants apparently do well in it.

KILLER QUESTIONS

I know what I want to do, but is there a market for it?

Market research

As the old military adage has it: *time spent in reconnaissance is seldom wasted.* Thus some research into the potential is perhaps a necessary preliminary.

SMART
ANSWERS
TO TOUGH
QUESTIONS

Q: What can market research do for me?

A: Overall the answer is simple: it can act to reduce business risk. More specifically, to quote the book *Market Research* (from Capstone's innovative 'ExpressExec' series), it has five key uses:

- Identify the size, shape and nature of a market, so as to understand the market and marketing opportunities.
- Investigate the strengths and weaknesses of competitive products and the level of trade support a company enjoys.
- Test out strategic and product ideas which help to define the most effective customer led strategies.
- Monitor the effectiveness of strategies.
- Help to define when marketing expenditure, promotions and targeting need to be adjusted or improved.

The variety of purpose listed above makes it clear that market research is not simply a 'first check'. It is useful ahead of any action, but it also provides a means of checking and refining views as operations proceed. Companies, especially those for which budgets always seem tight, who have selected one of these uses for market research are always concerned to make the research a worthwhile investment. Best results come when their marketing and sales planning is influenced by the results of research. In other words, when research pays for itself by providing a basis for change and improvement in operational matters.

You may not need a formal research survey, certainly not if you plan to work independently, but at the very least some desk research is called for. This can reassure you that there is a volume of work out there of

Desk research

The systematic collection and analysis of secondary data, which has been published, and existing information about markets and products from whatever source.

which you can aim at accessing a slice. More particularly you may want to look at typical existing operators – competitors – and how they operate. It is useful to know the kinds of client that others attract, how they appear to go about their marketing and whether there are lessons to learn from them.

It may also be useful, and possible, to talk to some potential clients. If you have a clear idea of what they want, and how they want it delivered,

SMART
ANSWERS
TO TOUGH
QUESTIONS

Q: What do I need to know about competitors?

A: In some senses as much as possible, but a systematic way of approaching this is under the key headings of the classic marketing mix:

- Product: what range of services do they offer, where is their main business and also what do they not do?
- Price: what do they charge, do fees vary service by service and how do they handle the 'extras' (expenses, etc.)?
- Presentation: how do they describe themselves? Some of this information is public (advertising, brochures, etc.), some is more difficult to obtain (proposals, for instance).

In addition, it is worth talking to other consultants, those who operate in a similar way to you but are not competitive; it may then be useful to both parties to compare notes. Bear in mind that it may be difficult to get a straight answer about other people's fees.

then this may help colour your own plans. So too will bearing in mind the length of assignment you are aiming for; this relates directly to how many clients you need. Finally, you want to investigate the more logistical aspects. For instance, you might aim to work primarily locally. If so, do you know how many organisations of a size and type that might be potential clients there are in your chosen radius? Do you know how many other consultants operate in the same area? Getting a handle on this may take only a visit to a commercial library.

Incidentally, research – or at the very least a close and objective eye on your market – is an ongoing activity. Things change and you can quickly find you are out of touch with the real situation in the market and misdirecting your efforts as a result.

With this sort of information in mind you can move on to consider exactly how you regard, and thus describe, your own range of services.

Your service range

A degree of specialization seems to work best. Consider large firms of consultants: often their overall claim is to do 'anything' in their chosen area. This is the way a large accountancy practice will operate, for instance. They may go beyond financial matters too, claiming to be able to advise on most matters connected with running an efficient and successful business. As soon as range begins to spread in this kind of way, as soon as the word 'comprehensive' is included in their brochures, credibility can suffer. Potential clients say: 'Can they really do *all* that?' So, what happens? They adopt a divisionalized strategy in some way. They have different departments to do different things and the credibility of each is maintained.

The best approach is to define and describe a range of services that can be understood and that will work in a number of tangible ways. For some people this is very tightly defined: they effectively only do one thing. This may work well, though it can make you vulnerable, and if the market declines for that one service it leaves a nasty hole. More often a range is involved. In defining range you need to consider:

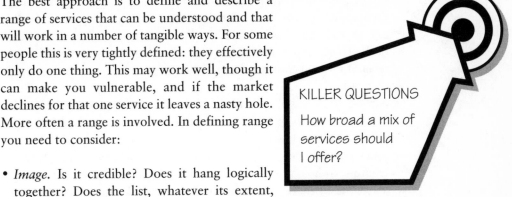

KILLER QUESTIONS

How broad a mix of services should I offer?

- *Image.* Is it credible? Does it hang logically together? Does the list, whatever its extent, hide the emphasis wanted on something that is to be a main element of the business? If you end up with a hotch-potch of disparate services that are difficult to describe and seem not to relate one to another, then some rationalization may be necessary. There may be things you are prepared to do, but which do not feature large. There may be areas where a real clash is possible. For example, few people who run public training events are involved in recruitment work because clients might feel (despite reassurances) that people attending could be put on a register and end up being encouraged to leave them. It is here, at least in part, that thinking about service range and overall strategy and positioning must come together. You need a clear view not only of what sort of operation you want to conduct, but how you want it to be perceived and where it will fit into the market. As a small operator the things that go with your service range (exceptional service, specially tailored approaches, etc.) are as important as anything else.

- *Synergy.* Some things hang naturally together. This may be either from a work point of view, two types of work linking to form one project, or it may involve your own marketing. In other words if you do one sort of work for a client then they are inherently open to talking to you about other activity. For instance, a graphic designer dealing with brochures might logically offer a copywriting service (even if they subcontract the work – see below)

- *Extension.* In order to build the business you may want to link main areas of work to other, subsidiary areas. In training, for instance, I concentrate on marketing, sales and communications skills (with some management matters as well), but simply by virtue of being regarded as having expertise in training I get asked about other topics. Some of these I am organized to undertake through associates. Effort to create this sort of situation may be worthwhile both commercially and in terms of client service, but a string of 'other things' could distract from the main message (and act to dissipate your efforts)

- *Omissions.* It is as important to decide what you will firmly reject as any part of your service. It is important to keep off areas where you have insufficient competence or experience to deal with them (or even to work with associates) because it will cloud your marketing. Also, undertaking an assignment that then fails to play to your strengths and delivers poor value can obviously be a disaster.

This last point is worth emphasizing. Do not get distracted by a long list of 'bits' that 'might be useful'. Concentrate of whatever you decide is your core range, and be as firm about including things out as you are about including others in.

What you want

While, as was made clear earlier, any service offered must make sense in the market, one of the advantages of being a consultant is to be able to do work you enjoy and find satisfying. Thus what you want is part of the equation here. You need to think through the intentions you have, see how they fit with the market opportunity and try to evolve a way of working that is satisfactory in both respects.

Everyone, and every area of work, will be different. That said, maybe the mix I have evolved illustrates the thinking here. I think of, and organize and promote, my work in a number of different 'categories'. These overlap in some ways but the list that follows should make sense:

- *Training* – this is the major part of my work. Topics aside, it falls into a number of areas, including in-company courses, public seminars and the preparation of training materials which others will deliver (e.g. for a course to be conducted many times around a large organization).

- *Consultancy* – again the nature of work varies. Some is close to training, as is one-to-one counselling. Other assignments may be in the area of strategic help, market research or more.

- *Overseas* – this is more likely to be training than consultancy and, while I have travelled widely, is concentrated in certain geographic areas (it is easier to create a flow of work if you visit regularly). This is, for me, an interesting area of work, occasionally overlaps with holiday plans, and adds in some ways to the overall image I project. Besides a week in Singapore in, say, a miserable British February is very nice.

- *Writing* – I write books, articles and training materials (and, more recently, for websites). I also do some copywriting. This can be done at home and makes a nice contrast with my training work which is, by definition, very people intensive. The other work provides the knowledge and examples that I need to be able to write.

Such a mix varies the work pattern. One activity can compliment another. It can work well in terms of productivity too: it would be difficult to schedule a training event every day of the year (exhausting too!), but having a writing project on the go to slot into the 'spare' time works well. Another focus many consultants work with is that of industry or product: a specialization in one field (or indeed several) can make work that much easier to sell.

You may want to target your chosen mix specifically, deciding in your plan how much revenue will come from each segment of your work. This will, in turn, affect your marketing and promotional activity.

Such a mix also relates closely to sales and marketing activity. Clearly in my list above different action is necessary to set up work overseas than in the UK or in one industry rather than another. Again the mix, the time scales involved and so on creates variety and interest.

I am not trying to sell you on any aspect of my mix. I am suggesting that a well thought-out mix can work well for you. It can add interest, variety and secure profitability. Nothing is of course forever. Such a mix is dynamic and you need to review it regularly to check that it still works effectively, that no change is necessary and particularly that no new events demand that changes are made.

Describing the service

A final point here. You must be able to describe your business in a way that can be got over clearly and easily, and that prompts a positive view. Sometimes a mixture of things can be encapsulated perfectly well, though maybe with one or two things taking a subsidiary role. On other occasions the mix is hopelessly incongruous and must be changed in some way to allow easy description.

How this is done can itself vary. I know consultants who work in strangely contrasting areas and simply split the two, in some cases virtually running two businesses in parallel. They may have two business cards, letterheads and brochures, and make this work.

Even a well-designed mix is inherently more difficult to cement in clients' minds than one simple service. You tend to get typecast. People I do training work for are most likely to think of me as a trainer; those I do consulting work for may think of me only with that hat on. There is a constant job of reinforcement to be done here, and again the dangers of too broad or disparate a list of services are obvious. On the other hand the precise mix you adopt is a part of what differentiates you from others, and that is worth bearing in mind too as you crystallize this area.

One more thing: most people who work in consultancy want to extend, and perhaps change, what they do to avoid undue repetition. It is simply more interesting to take on different kinds of things. You must pace yourself carefully and not leap so far at a time that quality of work suffers (or you find that to get something right, time spent increases and profitability declines).

> Honesty is important – tell the client if you have not done a particular type of work before or if you are not an expert. They will appreciate your honesty and integrity and trust will grow. Chances are, if you are keen and offer a sensible price – they will be happy for you to learn how on their assignment.
>
> Kim Tasso, independent marketing consultant and journalist

Therefore you may want to influence the mix of work progressively: though be careful not to concentrate on any fringe area or personal whim, however important what it might lead to in the long term, to the exclusion of executing work in your core area – and make sure there is sufficient of it to do.

The best way to predict the future is to invent it.

Dennis Gabor

You must *create* your business, and doing so demands you think through what you will do, and do not simply respond to every opportunity. This need not be unduly time consuming, but is worthwhile – a clear view of your business in this regard is a solid foundation from which to move ahead.

Having decided what services to offer, indeed having set up a way of viewing the dynamics of this in the longer term, you need to decide what fees to charge. It is to this we turn in the next chapter.

3

Setting Fees and Fee Policy

Consultancy may be inseparable from the word advice, but there is a difference. Advice can be freely given, but consultancy needs to be paid for. If you aim to work as a consultant, then you need to decide how exactly you will charge and, in due course, get the money due. I remember being told many years ago 'It is not a sale until the money is in the bank.' Very true; and I particularly called it to mind as I set up my own business.

This chapter is not going to recommend how much you charge. I know consultants who charge very different amounts, with the highest level being more than ten times the lower, and who seem content with the way it works for them. Rather it sets out to review how you decide how much to charge and look at the basis on which this is done and the way you implement your charging policy.

KILLER QUESTIONS

How much do
I charge for
my services?

Deciding the Basis of your Charges

Before we think about the level of charge that is appropriate, consider the overall basis of charge. There are three main bases:

- *By project.* Here the project is described in a proposal and the charge reflects doing the job. It presupposes that you can calculate accurately the time that the project will take. It also means that proposals need to state very clearly exactly what is involved. If you do not specify something, and it may be something as simple as progress meetings with the client, then you may find that client demands make the time this part of the project takes escalate. This can quickly lead to diluted profitability. That said, there are projects that this method suits and there are clients that simply demand to have work quoted this way. Time is inherent, but is not specifically mentioned, other than in terms of deadlines for completion of stages and ultimately of the overall project.

- *By time.* The most common way of charging is by time, usually by the hour or day. Sometimes the time is straightforward to calculate and quote for, indeed it is apparent to everyone. A simple example is my training work. If I conduct a two-day training course, clients expect to see a charge for those two days (and any investigation or preparatory time needs setting out, and agreeing, separately). Thus a project may be quoted specifically: so many days at such and such a rate, or it may necessitate some degree of imprecision. In other words you might need to say that something will take between X and Y days, in which case the cause of the imprecision needs to be spelt out.

- *By results.* This is rather different and the results need carefully specifying. However, though this is less common, an increasing number of projects are charged for on the basis of results. This might be linked to how much a project reduces costs for the client, or increases profit. It might also be linked to a deadline, a premium being paid if something successfully hits a tight completion date. Clearly the nature of the work affects this. Again there are simple examples: a number of public seminar providers pay the consultants who lead events on a scale linked to the number of participants who attend – more people, more revenue and the consultant gets a higher fee (and may also be more disposed to help with the promotion).

Q: Do my fees have to relate solely to one set basis?

A: No. They can be time or project related, the time frame can vary from an hour (or some minimum period you select) to a month or longer, as may be suitable if any of your work is more like interim management.

SMART
ANSWERS
TO TOUGH
QUESTIONS

There is no reason why elements of all of these cannot operate together, as indeed they do with the public seminar example which is, in effect, based on a fee per day that varies by results. Big projects can be complex in this regard, though the consultant must be sure that complexities, especially any insisted on or suggested by the client, do not lead to overlooking possible downsides that might remove some or all of the project's profitability.

With these factors in mind we now turn to deciding the level of fee that should be charged.

Deciding the level of your charges

Assuming you do not just pick a figure out of a hat (not recommended) you need to think through what you might charge. There are four factors to bear in mind here; none can be the sole basis of the decision, but all do have a bearing on the end result. There are some circumstances where the client dictates. I have worked for management bodies, for instance, where they have a standard fee for training work and, in effect, say *take it or leave it*. Now it is said that everything is negotiable, so this may need that kind of response. Alternatively the four factors now investigated can be used to assess the benefit of accepting such a deal, as well as setting your own offering.

Cost plus pricing

The first factor is based, simplistically, on assessing your costs and adding a margin for profit. This means assessing your overall costs in working as a consultant. List them, and make sure you leave nothing out. In no special order, such costs are likely to include:

• Telephone (fixed and mobile)

• Postage

• Stationary and printing

- Insurance

- Benefits (health insurance)

- Travel (including your car)

- Research (everything from networking to magazine subscriptions)

- Accounting and banking (including any loans)

- Promotion and selling costs

- Office (which might be in your home)

- Secretarial or other support costs

- Equipment (and maintenance costs – including computer and computer upgrades)

You may well be able to think of other smaller, though significant, headings; indeed if you cannot work this out you should perhaps consider whether you have the skills consultancy demands! *Note:* you need to consider too what costs you will charge to your clients and what proportion of your costs you will get paid this way.

If you are just setting up in business, you may also have to cover set-up costs and need to decide how, and how quickly, to do that.

You also need to consider the proportion of your time that will be fee earning. Realistically you need time to run the business, to keep up to date and prepare and, not least, to sell and set up assignments. You may also want some holiday (writing books gives me some royalty income not linked to the time the work is done, so I tell myself I earn something on holiday – but I am digressing now).

This done, you can work out a number of things: primarily the minimum fee that will cover the costs, and the fee level necessary to earn what you want (you might sensibly set a target) in the number of 'fee days' you reckon you will work. It remains to be seen whether the outcome of this is practical – your target could be so high no one will pay so much – but with the facts from this analysis in mind you can consider, in parallel, the next factor.

SMART VOICES

In the management consulting business, consulting firms normally set their fees at 2.2 times the consultants' cost, figuring that this will cover their total costs and leave an attractive margin.

Philip Kotler, in *Kotler on Marketing* (Free Press)

Demand pricing

This factor looks externally at the market place. Simplistically, high demand means that it is possible to charge high prices. For example, in technical areas if there is a definite shortage of people with the required expertise, then if you are such an expert you will find this factor alone allows you to be more bullish about the fees that you charge.

You need to be realistic. Do you do something unique? Or do your potential clients have plenty of choice as it is a competitive area that you operate in? It is possible that the answer is different in different parts of the range of services you offer and you will find yourself working at a range of different fee levels. This is common enough, but means that you need to consider the mix and be sure that not all your work is in sectors that only allow the lowest of your range of charges to be made.

Remember here the nature of precedent. If you are in the early stages of setting up, you may be tempted to start with lower fees to make getting going easier. Even if it has this effect, remember that it is going to be difficult to say to clients next time that you want half as much again.

Competition pricing

The next thing is to examine 'going rates'. What are other people charging? This is not entirely easy. Many consultants, and consulting firms, do work at a wide range of fee levels; for example, these may link to the nature of the work and the level (and thus experience) of the consultant working on it. However, you can probably get some idea, from published sources, from networking or research with other consultants and, not least, from clients. Given that the range is wide you still have to decide how best to position yourself, but it is a start. *Note:* it is worth taking steps to keep your external view up to date, things change and it is easy over time to find that you are charging last year's rates if you do not maintain an external view.

Marketing (or value) based pricing

Price and quality go together. With any product, people use price to judge its appropriateness for them. Consider anything you might buy personally. Shoes, a computer, a car – in any case such as this you probably have a cost you will not go above (if only in some cases because you cannot afford it). But you may well have a price you would be wary of going below as well. Think about it. Those shoes may be low cost, but how long would they look smart or last? With some products appearance is important also – you do not want to be seen driving round in a rusting Ford Cortina, however much money it may save you.

So here you need to think about what your chosen fee level will *say about you.* Will it reinforce the professional image you are at pains to project? Overall there is probably a greater danger if too low a fee is selected than if too high a one is chosen; it is easier to come down than to negotiate up.

Smart things to say

Positioning

The balance you strike regarding your service (product), the way it is delivered (service), your price and marketing message. Positioning is less something you do to the product, rather what you put in the mind of your prospects.

The fee, realistically the fee range, you select will be linked by your clients and outside contacts to your:

- Professionalism

- Expertise

- Success

- Size (of your operation or firm)

- Style and way of operating

- Credibility and trustworthiness

- Certainty of delivering

Also important is your chosen profile – fees are part of your image (a point picked up in the next chapter). The nature of how an individual consultant wants to work varies enormously. At one end is the person who wants to work locally, perhaps without much travel and in an area away from a main city like London. Prevailing rates for such a consultant are probably comparatively low (but so may be costs), they may elect to operate at the high end of this but the overall restriction remains. Another person may aim to work as an international guru to major companies and anything but a high fee simply fails to project the right picture.

Realistically, you must bear the implications of all four of these main overall factors in mind in making your decisions. Your decisions need to put you in a manageable range: *Normally I will charge between X and Y per day.* They also need to signal the proportion of your work that needs to be at different rates. And this may have further implications because it relates also to the range of different services you offer, the different kinds of work you do and the different kinds of organization you need as clients.

SMART
ANSWERS
TO TOUGH
QUESTIONS

Q: How do I monitor how my pricing policy is working?

A: Realistically you will probably work at a number of different fee levels, or different 'day-rates' depending on the work and the client. It is easy to make exceptions, cutting price a little here and there for what may seem all sorts of good reasons. But overall profitability can easily suffer. Keep a running average of your key fee measure (day-rate, say) and use this to monitor progress; if your average is consistently below your intention, something needs to change.

One more thing: there are certain kinds of work where the price is set by the client. This is so in my business with certain public seminar operators. If you want to conduct a course for them, you must accept the going rate. Some negotiation may be possible in these circumstances, especially after some initial success, and there may be details, e.g. expenses, you can influence which affect profitability. But there are occasions when the only decision is to accept the policy or not; though you might want to comment, positioning it as an exception perhaps, so as to make your position clear. Just occasionally I have come across situations when the 'take it or leave it price' is *more* than you expect, perhaps more than you would have asked for. Resist the temptation to allow your pleasure to show, and do not automatically rule out any negotiation – perhaps you can make it better still.

Having decided what to charge, you need to apply and describe those charges to projects and clients. Before considering that, there are a number of details to be considered, indeed to keep in mind.

Detailed implementation factors

The following areas contain both pitfalls and opportunities. The challenge is to make everything under all of these headings work well; and that means making them maximize your profitability and yet ensure clients see the way you operate as reasonable, clear and acceptable. First, some definitions:

Defining terms   You need to be clear about some basic terminology. For example:

- *What is a 'day'?* You might regard this as eight hours, or more or less. You also need to consider breaks such as lunch

- *Hourly rates.* Again you need to think about this – is it the day rate divided by eight (and rounded up or down to give a round or right-sounding figure)? Or does a full day cost less per hour than smaller commitments?

- *Minimum commitment.* Decisions are necessary here too. One day

SMART ANSWERS TO TOUGH QUESTIONS

might well make sense, but what about one hour? You may need a minimum commitment, but you may need to be prepared to vary this on the basis of different clients and circumstances

- *Travel time.* It used to be the norm for this to be charged for, often at the same rate as work. This seems increasingly not to be the case. Client pressure dictates more flexibility, so often a lower rate is agreed or a nominal amount added to cover travel time that does not relate exactly to the actual journey time. This is something else to be clear about ahead of making proposals.

SMART QUOTES

Expenses It has always been, and remains, the norm for some expenses to be charged and these can include: travel in all its forms, hotel accommodation, postage, printing, hire of equipment (anything from presentational aids to a meeting room), advertising (as with recruitment work), and even temporary staff (for research work, perhaps). Expenses may well be an inevitable consequence of the assignment, but dealing with them needs some care. You should note the following:

- *Agree them in advance.* This is vital, and no single item listed on your invoice should surprise, certainly not cause questions of concern. This means that the detail of such things as class of rail or air travel, type of hotel booked and so on should be checked and agreed in advance. Many people would say this means having it in writing.

- *Organize it so that they pay up front.* If your client wants you to fly somewhere, then you need to charge them the, agreed, airfare. It may be better, however, if they book it and send you the ticket. This means the charge can go direct to them and this helps your cash flow. It may also mean they can take advantage of corporate discounts and that you get the advantage of any special deals (maybe they use one hotel group and have negotiated an automatic room upgrade).

- *Organize it so that you have control.* This might be better than the idea it follows. If you have a frequent-flier card, book your flight in the right way, then maybe that gets you a free flight quicker and helps reduce holiday costs. Decide which is best for you and push for it, but never push things that the client might end up resenting. If you are always seen to be acting in their best interests it may win you some points.

- *Document as necessary.* This goes with the way you agree things, but if you are asked for a significant receipt, then make sure you have it.

- *Never be extravagant.* There will sometimes be costs you incur in the course of an assignment that cannot be recharged; it is simply inappropriate. Such includes items that are purely for your convenience, the charge for a movie channel in a hotel might be an example. It is worth playing it safe as this is the worst category of thing to fall out with a client over. Indeed some consultants like to make a point about this sort of item to illustrate that there need be no fear they will run up inappropriate costs – *for example, I never charge alcoholic drinks to a hotel bill.*

A little thought in this area can make sure you are not unnecessarily out of pocket, yet ensure also that a client never has cause to complain. Remember that clients are different and take different attitudes to things. Using their systems may be one way of helping this whole process. For example, I usually ask a client what mileage rate it uses internally and abide by that – some are probably more, some less than any standard rate I might go for. It makes little financial difference, but is a gesture that says *I'm being careful and reasonable.*

I know of one occasion when a consultant had to make a rail journey with the Managing Director of an organization with which he was working. As they walked along the platform together, the consultant boarded a first-class carriage. The MD had a second-class ticket; indeed, he explained that no one in the company travelled first class. While travel costs had been detailed and agreed in the original proposal, the type of ticket was not mentioned. The MD took the view that this was sharp practice and the following day he cancelled what was a substantial assignment halfway through. It pays to think ahead, and to check.

Note: Being careful to record expenses and keep receipts will reduce your costs through tax and reclaiming VAT, even if they cannot be charged to a client.

Terms and conditions   Make these clear. Key things to set out and agree are payment terms, and what happens if assignments are curtailed or cancelled (the latter as much as an incentive not to do it as to recoup finances if it is done). Stage payments, often with something up front (e.g. on agreement to proceed or on commencement), are largely the norm for assignments spanning any real amount of time and also protect you against last-minute cancellations (they may mean that, in effect, you already have the cancellation fee in your bank).

Taxes   It is a small point perhaps, but make sure that all discussions and written statements of expenses make clear how tax will be dealt with (in the United Kingdom expenses must have VAT added to them, and not every client organization can claim this back)

Proposals   Writing proposals is dealt with in a separate chapter, here in context of fees it is worth mentioning as a source of extra revenue. Not always, of course, but sometimes some of the time of preparing and submitting a proposal can be charged for. Either it can be built into the

Q: Do I need a contractual arrangement with my clients?

A: You probably have one on the basis that even a verbal agreement of something can constitute a contract. A simple exchange of letters may suffice, as may the terms and conditions listed in your proposal (and you may elect to get a copy of this signed and returned by the client).

Having clear contractual arrangements can:

- Prevent misunderstandings (provided they are clearly communicated)
- Project efficiency and enhance client relationships
- Link to other formalities of arrangement and documentation.

You need to evolve a straightforward way of introducing the concept and making it acceptable (do not just say 'Sign here'). So:

- Take the initiative and introduce the concept of a contractual arrangement.
- Spell out the detail you suggest/want clearly and ask if they wish to add to it.
- Stress particularly any figures and timing issues.
- Check the client understands and agrees.
- Document the arrangement.
- Ask, specifically, for their confirmation (this might entail signing a form or exchanging letters).
- Keep clear records of what you have done and make sure all documents are filed carefully (you may never need this, but if you do it will be important).
- Chase for action if necessary (and think carefully about actually starting work with anything outstanding).
- Make sure that throughout the process you strike the right note about it: make it clear this is a practical matter that is in the interests of both parties.
- Link everything done to the administration of the assignment (you will look silly — and annoy — if your invoice does not match with the contractual basis for invoicing, for example).

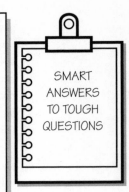

SMART ANSWERS TO TOUGH QUESTIONS

project cost, or specifically agreed as a cost, payable whether work proceeds or not. If the tailoring of a proposal demands meetings, travel to several locations, research or just takes time – then some of that may be charged to the client. You may want to suggest this is a 'nominal', though significant, amount or charge at a set proportion of your core fee (two-thirds of the stated day rate, say). In some areas of work this sort of thing is the norm, in others it may need approaching carefully. It is especially likely to be agreed if some element of the cost is dictated by the client; if, for example, they insist you visit someone in a far-flung office, then, at the very least, you might succeed in getting them to pay the travel cost.

Invoices   Like any other document that you send to a client, invoices need to look professional. Check and double-check the calculations; it is embarrassing to have someone telephoning to say *You can't add up and you've charged us too much*. In addition make sure:

- They are clear and understandable.

- They correspond *exactly* with what was agreed.

- The payment terms and method are clear.

- Any client procedures are adhered to (for instance quoting a purchase order).

Beyond that, always send them out on time. And always follow them up at once if payment is not received by the due date. Cash flow is important for both parties, and most organizations will delay payment if they can. Leave off a purchase order and many a client will use the fact to delay payment. Do not allow a situation where your invoice languishes on a pile marked *Not chased yet, leave payment a bit longer*. Even in a small business, money saved is almost as good as money earned, and if you invoice to minimize the bank charges that a poor cash flow may run up, it is one more thing on the side of profitability.

Fee increases   Fee increases, in common with any sort of price increase, are never welcomed by any customer. Yet they are necessary and it is all too easy to fall behind. The moral is clear: first make it clear in proposals how far ahead fee levels are guaranteed, and secondly increase fees regularly. This normally means once a year, and this means that the fee increase need not be great or seen as a problem. Leave it two or three years and the percentage you will then need to add to maintain the situation will seem excessive – *How much?* – and may well meet with resistance. A little and often approach usually makes most sense.

Charging for overseas work   Two factors are important here. You have to find out about the market rate. What are people paying for services like yours in another country? If it is much less than your charges, either you have to match it (or get near) or you have to be very sure you offer something special and can make a case for it being worth a premium. Having said that, there is an area of international work where the rate paid applies across country boundaries, for instance in the way a multinational company might commission work to be done in a variety of

SMART
ANSWERS
TO TOUGH
QUESTIONS

Q: Can I ever specify payment in cash?

A: Rarely, I suspect, but it may be possible and desirable, for example, for a one-off assignment in an overseas market where chasing a bad debt, or even financing a long wait, might then be avoided. Writing this reminds me of one course I conducted for an organization overseas. Payment had not been specified in any particular way and at the end of the first day of the programme I was solemnly handed an envelope in which was half my fee. At the end of the second and final day the process was repeated!

countries and pay the same rate for it all. If you work for a national organization, however, then it may be different and they want value for money in their terms.

This may preclude work in some areas, but if you work in English there is still a good deal of the world to regard as your market. One point: you need to balance the fact that most people like prices quoted in their currency with the possibility of foreign currency fluctuations. For large amounts of work you can catch a real cold if rates change; for shorter assignments you may be seen as taking a market more seriously if you charge in the local currency.

Describing price

Whatever fee level you settle on, you need to present it right. This is investigated further in Chapters 7 and 8. Here we set the scene and concentrate on the presentational aspect, mentioning just two important factors.

Make it clear

The first rule is to achieve clarity. This sounds obvious, but a subtle compromise is necessary here. The fee might be stated as one bald figure; alternatively it might be made more palatable. For example, some people recommend listing staged projects with a price per stage but with no total shown. Fees and expenses may be listed separately. At one extreme it becomes complicated for clients to work out total costs (something that is made worse by any necessary estimates that may be involved), at the other the total cost jumps out unencumbered – and may shock. What is best here varies depending on the nature of the input being priced, and always needs some consideration.

A particular thing about which to exercise care concerns extras. If there are factors that might increase or change, these need to be listed. A project might, for example, schedule a number of meetings. If that, or anything else, could change, then this needs to be raised, agreed and documented. When the invoice is delivered, clients should not be wondering why it is different from original estimates; they should know. Too much information here is always better than too little, and some clients may invoke the letter of the law, as it were, if work simply expands – *It was your decision to change that, if it took longer then that's your problem.*

Psychological impact

The way people see, and assess, price may seem odd in some respects. For example, we are used to seeing items at prices such as £9.99 in stores of all sorts. Why? Because there is a great deal of research to show that people buy more at this level than at £10. In some ways it matters not why people think this way, it is simply a fact to be used. So, consider:

Round figures
Because of the situation described above, which is similar right up the scale of price, it is usually prudent to avoid quoting fees in round figures. At one level £995 is perceived as *significantly* less than £1,000. Other major prices – £10,000, £50,000 and so on – can be viewed in a similar way. This can apply to day rates and to project costs.

There is a very important additional element here with regard to consultancy. It is, by its nature, bespoke. If a client poses a specific problem, then they ask for a *tailored* approach to the work they seek to assist tackle it. They view themselves as individuals, which they are, and they regard their situation as unique (whereas you may see it as very similar to other situations you have seen elsewhere). Tell them that you have worked out a unique approach solely for them and that it just happens that the work will cost £10,000 and it is unlikely to sound credible. They will either infer that it is a standard approach rather than something tailored, or they will believe it is tailored and the fee has been calculated and then rounded up. Either way this does the likelihood of selling, especially in a competitive arena, no good at all.

Odd in some ways, but worthy of note.

Smart things to say

Price must always suggest value for money and, where appropriate, indicate that the solution is tailor-made.

Range Sometimes work cannot be quoted for in terms of an exact figure. You have to say that it will be between X and Y. Just using round figures, a range such as between £10,000 and £12,000 may seem acceptable, whereas a range of £6,000–12,000 is simply seen as vague and unhelpful; the gap is *too* wide. Choose a sensible range and take pains to explain exactly why there is a gap of a certain size that must be involved. In other words make very clear those aspects of the assignment that cannot be stated more precisely at this stage.

It may also be worth making clear where the work or the consultant dictates the imprecision and where the client does. For example, the client may want regular review meetings, but be undecided just how many make sense or where they will be.

We will later return to those aspects of price and fees that help, or hinder, the sales process. In Chapter 9 we link to the systems that enable us to control price levels and profitability.

One final point: if you find yourself negotiating price, this needs doing with care. Remember that your proposals are your first recommendation: *This is how I suggest you tackle this.* So, if the client demands cost reduction and you suggest dropping or abbreviating Stage Three, then they may wonder why it was suggested in the first place if it can now so easily be dropped. Credibility can suffer at an important early stage in the relationship. If changes are made, then they must be accompanied by explanations about how results, accuracy or timing may be affected. In other words a reduced price buys something different. Again care is necessary.

Overall there is probably more likelihood of problems coming from understating fees than taking a bullish view, and many consultants take the view that *if you haven't lost an assignment lately because your price was too high, then you are not charging enough.* Conversely, if you are busy, it is a good time to experiment with a few higher quotations.

Client: What I want to hire is a one-armed consultant.

Consultant: How so?

Client: Because it would stop then from always saying *On the one hand I recommend this, on the other hand . . .*

SMART QUOTES

4

Image and Profile

There is an old saying from the marketing world that 'Perception is reality'. With this in mind, think about the process of hiring a consultant from the clients' point of view. They have to pick someone to talk to. They may meet you at an event and then request a meeting, or they may see a variety of details from a number of consultants and from an assessment of that decide on one, or a short list, to talk to in the first instance. They may meet you following a recommendation, and it is just as important to present the right image to those who might recommend you as to those you want as clients.

Whatever may lead up to it, there is usually a meeting, an exchange of business cards, a look at brochures and, if matters go further, they may request and get a proposal, or ask for and be given a formal presentation. Discussions may include reference to past work, actual recommendations or statements from referees. But whatever is done, and however much checking out goes on, the next step is, to some degree, a shot in the dark.

In effect, what consultants do is ask someone to choose, commit and quite possibly pay some money up front – *and then find out if they are any good or not*. It is a fact of life, and a topic revisited in other ways in Chapter 7, that services of this sort *cannot be tested*. Past good work does not *guarantee* that the next assignment will be well executed. Consultancy is not like buying a suit. The client cannot try it on, feel the material or see if it matches their shoes. They must trust you, and their own judgement.

Given the fact that they cannot actually test the service, they are wary (suspicious?) and will try to assess anything and everything that they believe, or hope, will give them a sign and reduce the risk that they take in hiring you.

> ## SMART QUOTES
>
> A consultant is a person with their tongue in your ear, their hand on your wallet and their faith in your gullibility.
>
> Anon. (traditional clients' view)

The whole area of image is important here. You must work to see that everything about how you appear and operate contributes to your employment being seen as desirable.

It is an area of cumulative effect. They do not look at, say, a business card, and think *What an excellent design, I bet this guy is good*, but they do form an increasingly tangible view from all the ways in which you progressively come over during these early stages of contact. An important one is initial meetings – usually sales meetings – and, as we will see in Chapter 7, how these are conducted is always important to how you are seen. All the details matter, and it is the sum total at the end of the day that prompts action; or does not. Given the competitive nature of the consulting market, you cannot afford to have gaps in your image armoury.

So, the result of all this is unavoidable. You need to decide on the kind of image that you want to project, then create and maintain it.

The professional image you want

You doubtless want to be seen as *professional*. Fine, but what does this mean exactly? Ask yourself what your clients would expect of someone like you – what qualities and characteristics would make them say *They're professional*. Some of these will be common factors and some examples are given here alongside some of the ways in which a positive view of them can be generated. You may feel you need to appear:

- *Experienced.* You may need to have examples of work done to hand (and well documented so that you can volunteer relevant examples and details).

- *Expert.* In part perhaps from looking the part, more so by being able to talk in the right way (to show that you understand an industry, say) and quote examples of what you have done in the past (your facility to do this might usefully be augmented by a good database – see page 98).

- *Well qualified.* This could literally mean qualifications – everything from an MBA to a technical qualification in, say, engineering – or it might refer to other abilities such as speaking a foreign language fluently. There is an overlap here with

KILLER QUESTIONS
How do I want people
especially potential
and actual clients,
to see me and think
about me?

experience – some clients list having certain experience as what qualifies someone to work with them

- *Well organized.* this must show, and it is worth taking up early opportunities to demonstrate it; this applies even to simple matters such as confirming the details of a meeting

- *Looking the part.* See page 61.

- *Sincere, honest and trustworthy.* This will probably be assumed unless you give signs to the contrary, however you can indicate it obliquely, for instance by *offering* to supply references

- *Confident.* Sometimes this needs to be evident externally more than it is felt internally; but it must never deteriorate into arrogance, people are quickly switched off if you are condescending and talk down to them. (You *do know* what condescending means don't you? Sorry, irresistible.)

- *Tactful.* One way of demonstrating this is by the way you refer to such things as confidentiality.

- *A good communicator.* This should be in evidence early on and throughout your relationship with a client. You should have no weak links, being fine in a one-to-one meeting, say, but less so in a presentation or a report

- *Reliable.* You may be able to indicate the importance you place on this, but ultimately clients will judge you by what they get

- *Knowledgeable.* Clients do not expect you to be omniscient (well, not usually!) but they do expect evidence of knowledge of your specialist area and often of their situation to some extent (for example, they may want you to know their industry or product and equally may test this somewhat).

- *Well prepared.* This should always be in evidence – try never to say things like 'What was it you said about X?' (make notes), always have the relevant papers with you (and be familiar with them) and so on. This is both a courtesy and a practical consideration.

- *To give attention to detail.* It is good if they think of you as missing nothing, it may also be useful if you relate to the individual client in this area – some may be most concerned with the broad picture, others will want every i dotted and every t crossed.

Q: Is there a danger that trying too hard to project a professional image will look contrived?

A: Could be, but the examples given of desirable characteristics (and most anything you could add) are essentially sensible. You should not have to persuade yourself that it is worthwhile to appear well prepared, say. You need to be able to do whatever you need to do to make it so. The suggestion beyond that is only that you keep half an eye on the visibility of such a thing. For example, just saying 'Knowing of your interest in X, I prepared some information about Y for you' rather than just using the information without comment gives a distinctly different – and improved – impression. Sometimes there may be things you elect to exaggerate a little, but there is no need to go over the top.

SMART
ANSWERS
TO TOUGH
QUESTIONS

- *Client focused.* Nothing gives the wrong impression quicker than displaying *any* sort of lack of interest in the client or anything they regard as important.

- *Efficient*: always be efficient and perhaps on occasion make it evident just how efficient you are.

Other characteristics will be more particular to any specialist field in which you work. An IT consultant might want to be seen not just as expert and up to date, for instance, but as good at communicating with less technical people if such were their typical client.

It is useful to be specific here: first, make a list of all those factors that you think make sense for you and your business. Then rate each item on the list. Where are you strong and where are you weak? For example, if you are older, then there is going to be little problem persuading people you have experience, whereas if you are younger you are going to have to take more steps to give your capabilities credibility.

SMART
ANSWERS
TO TOUGH
QUESTIONS

Q: How can I make my limited experience seem more impressive?

A: First, avoid lying and making things up (you will only be found out and it will become self-defeating). What you can do is quote 'corporate' experience. Thus if you are a small firm, or even if you work with associates on some basis, you can speak for the organization 'We have done . . .'. You may want to collect and catalogue matters that can be described in this way. Similarly careful phraseology may make you able to describe experiences in line management positions (if that is your background) in a way that is useful. Beyond that console yourself with the thought that, all too soon, you will grow out of the problem.

Appearance

Let us start with a well-known quotation . . .

It should be said at once that the objective here is
not to stereotype you or to remove anything of
real character and replace it by a universally bland
image. The days of the organization where every
businessman, for example, was expected to wear
the same (plain white shirt, grey suit, black shoes
and conservative tie) are largely gone, and dress
now involves a much wider range of acceptable options. Women too,
appearing on the corporate scene in larger numbers and more senior
positions than in the past, have wide choice. It is, however, a matter of
'horses for courses' and you need to consider what is suitable. Indeed
you need to consider what 'suitable' means.

Some things are universally only sensible. I will take the case of a man
(being one myself) just to allow some example: clean shoes, a well-
pressed suit and a smart tie may always be acceptable. But there are
exceptions. If a jacket and slacks is what is worn at a client's office, so be
it, then wearing that in a well-turned out way may be fine. Many consultants seem to feel that it is best to be just a tad smarter than the average
level in any low-formality environment.

On the other hand, there is no option but to make individual judgements. If you work for an advertising agency or some other creative
company, then a suit, particularly a conventional business suit, might be
regarded as wildly overdressed. Conversely, there may be a good deal to
be gained by being the only one in a more conservative group who dares
to wear a corduroy suit or a really jazzy tie, so that may be the right

action too – for some. The most important thing is to think about it. If you simply emerge bleary-eyed from bed and reach for whatever looks reasonably clean you may miss some tricks. The current trend for 'dressing down' and informal days is fine, but does make more decisions necessary.

There are things beyond clothes that need similar consideration.

What you have around you also speaks volumes about you. There are many things that you have about you that contribute to your overall image. Certainly your office is one major one. It acts as a kind of billboard to those seeking to form judgements about you.

Assuming you have a personal office, then signposts there include its:

- Location (e.g. penthouse or basement)

- Size

- Purpose (e.g. accommodating just you, or with a meeting table/chairs)

- Organization (e.g. tidy or bomb-site)

- Busyness (e.g. does it appear to be a place for work or relaxation?)

SMART VOICES

Samuel Gosling

These matters even have a scientific as well as a common-sense basis. Samuel Gosling from the University of Texas has researched the accuracy of inferring what people are like from the appearance of their personal work environment. The characteristics most easily discernible were conscientiousness and openness. See Journal of Personality and Social Psychology, vol. 82 for the details.

- Contents (e.g. computer and other equipment)

- Embellishments (e.g. pictures on the wall)

Your offices – premises – can be analysed in the same sort of way, so be sure they work hard to reinforce your desired image.

The situation is similar with regard to yourself and your more personal accoutrements. Here again there is no one right approach or single solution to how to deal with any particular area. A balance has to be struck, and you can usefully think about how your present way of working comes over in this respect. The following list is designed to get you thinking about the implications here, and perhaps prompt you to think of those factors that you can yourself adjust or arrange to help create the positive image you want.

- The best computer on your desk may be good, but can you work it?

- Are six email addresses making you look more important or pretentious?

- Is a fat Filofax best or a slim one?

- Does your electronic organizer really save you time, or will being seen to wipe out *all* of your telephone number list one day make you look less than efficient?

- Should certificates (such as for membership of a professional institute) be on show?

The totality of everything you gradually accumulate around you – including such things as your choice of company car, the hotels you stay in when away on business, even which class you travel on planes and trains – all play a part in creating the image you present to others. While you can certainly become too contrived about this sort of thing, it is likely to be worse to accord it too little consideration. Overall the one word that perhaps sums up the most suitable working environment for a consultant is businesslike. If you work from home you may go to clients far more than they visit you; when it does occur the other way round it is worth moving the cat off your computer before you show them into your study.

Enquirer: Can you come and have a meeting with me I have a project in mind that you might be able to help with?

Consultant (after asking various questions and agreeing a date): Are you talking to any other firms?

Enquirer: Well, I have talked to one consultant, but as he arrived at our offices in a Porsche I felt that getting another quotation would be sensible.

This paraphrases an enquiry received by the author a few years ago (sadly in some ways my car did not cause the same feeling; but I got the job). Incidentally, it is good practice to ask if you do face competition. People will not always say who, but surprise at being asked might lead to an honest answer, and you might then be able to better direct your proposals if you know the opposition.

Each factor is worth thinking about. For example, it is surely true that you are more likely to deliver appropriate results if you are well organized. Furthermore, you are more likely to be taken seriously if you are *seen to be* well organized. Consider some examples of practice that gives a positive impression:

- *Punctuality.* Turning up for things on time and hitting deadlines takes some effort, but is worthwhile in terms of the impression of efficiency it creates.

- *Time management.* Managing your time, your projects and diary and creating strong productivity is also well worthwhile. Good time management can increase productivity significantly. So, although there is no magic formula and the secret lies in the details and creating the right disciplines, becoming good in this way is really a necessity (see page 200).

- *Tidiness* – literally *looking* well organized. Your office, your desk, your paperwork and your briefcase all can assist you in putting over the image that you have decided upon. Preparation clearly helps.

Essential image generators

A number of specific factors are important in generating an image: two that are key are the name of your business and how you present it.

Business name

KILLER QUESTIONS

What name should
I trade under?

Here I will ignore the question of the legal issues of a business name, not because it is unimportant, but because the issues vary depending on the constitution of your firm and where you work. Certainly be careful in this area and avoid clashes with other businesses. What other considerations are there in choosing a name? There is certainly not one clear favourite route here, but the questions that need answering are common:

- *What should it say about size?* I could have opted to trade as *Patrick Forsyth Associates* but it seems to be this carries a clear 'small' label. I might have added the word *International* to the name I chose, but if you do that make sure you can claim it has a purpose. If 'overseas' means the Isle of Wight, then it may not be suitable and will, if queried, give the wrong impression.

- *What does it say about the nature of your business?* Indeed how much do you want it to say? More can be said as a 'subtitle' to a name on a business card or letterhead if you wish. Trying to inject too much description could lead to something unmanageable *Touchstone International Consultancy Training Research and Windowcleaning* – I think not.

- *Does a made-up word work well?* In other fields it has, e.g. *Kodak*

- *Should it be 'clever'?* A play on words perhaps, or something like the *Orbit* example on page 21.

- *Is picking an irrelevant association ruled out?* My address starts Saltcote Maltings so, as many people do, I could have chosen *Saltcote Consultants*. Personally I think this demonstrates nothing except a lack of imagination.

- *What about initials? PF Associates?* Again I do not particularly like this approach and certainly some sets of initials fail to trip lightly off the tongue. Also many companies have an 'initials name' following a change from a name that no longer encompassed their business; in such circumstances, keen not to throw the baby out with the proverbial bath water, it is an obvious route to take.

- *What about the 'solicitors' approach'?* Forsyth, Garratt, Jacks &

McTavish – may be awkward, and what happens when John Davies joins the partnership?

- *Is it practical?* Will people be able to pronounce it, how does it sound over the telephone, will the length fit on business cards, does it mean something rude in Scandinavia? These questions and more all need considering.

- *Is it in any sense fashionable and likely to date?* Here the same might be said of any design or logo that goes with it.

- *Will any necessary variants fit with it neatly?* Should I have a second name – *Touchstone Business Writing?*

- *Letterheads and business cards.* It is here that your chosen name will appear. In a service these are disproportionately important. They should look good. It is subjective, but professional help may create

Why *Touchstone Training & Consultancy?*

I rejected the 'Associates' route at the start as too likely to seem small (and insignificant?). I picked a name not used elsewhere in the area of work I undertake, a word with some meaning and that seemed to have some relevance. (According to the dictionary a touchstone is 'a standard or criteria against which other things are measured'. The word implies excellence and will, for some people, remind them of William Shakespeare.) A word that sounded okay (yes, a totally subjective feel) and which sounded okay also with the brief description of area of work offered by the firm and, as the firm is a partnership, presented it without any suffix such as Limited.

Like it or not (and I have only ever had positive comment) it is an example of how to think this vexed question through.

what you want. A good design is worth paying for; do not leave it to the package deal of the local print shop.

Two colours is surely essential: anything else looks cheap. Be practical – does it photocopy (pastel colours may be wrong), does any way in which the name or logo is presented look equally good in various sizes? Does a colour link easily to things like a standard binder cover? Choose a good paper (mine also has some embossing), and create something that is going to do a good job for you – after all, people will probably see more of this than anything else you send them.

One further point is well worth considering here. Once you make a decision you are stuck with it for some time, even changing your letterhead is not something to be done too often. So think long and hard and decide wisely. You can do a lot worse than try out ideas and designs on a few other people (and not those who will just say 'Lovely' to be nice) rather than trusting your own judgement alone – though ultimately you must decide

- *Promotional material.* This must look good and read well and must match in style the tone set with basic materials such as letterheads This area is considered in detail in Chapter 6.

Appearance – in all its manifestations – should not be dismissed as cosmetic irrelevance. It is an area well worth some thought. There are few rules as to how to proceed, other than that you need to work at it and take and implement a series of considered judgements to get the balance right. If people are going to see you as influential, as a power to be reckoned with in whatever way and to whatever degree you want, then the sum total of the many ways in which others perceive you must be designed to work actively for you. The objective is to directly influence how people relate to you. Simplistically, this means that if you look like a doormat, you tend to get trodden on, and if you appear to have clout, the respect you command increases.

The ultimate image enhancer

The image that you put over for yourself and your firm is contributed to by many things (certainly in Chapters 6, 7 and 8, which look at promotion and sales, image will be seen as underlying all that is said there). However smart and professional your letterhead or anything else of that sort, there is one influence that always outweighs everything else.

That is you.

The way you conduct yourself is vital. It is important in making first contacts and throughout the relationship with a client. It is important with people you know well, and have perhaps worked for often over a period of time, and it is important with people you have just met. It is important with networking contacts, intermediaries and others who may recommend you, and it is important with past, present and future clients. Everything you do to get work and everything you do to conduct work says something about you. It is an active process that makes sure that what is says is not simply positive, but that it is business generating – making it more likely that you get work, keep work and expand your client relationships.

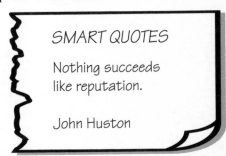

SMART QUOTES

Nothing succeeds like reputation.

John Huston

Once people know you, then the job is to reinforce a good initial impression and add detail in the way you consider most valuable.

In summary here, always remember that:

- You only get one chance to make a good first impression (it may be a cliché, but it is true).

- The details matter and contribute to the total effect (for good or ill).

- As has been said, perception really *is* reality, people really will judge you on appearances.

- Consistency of overall approach helps to build an image cumulatively so, 'it pays to advertise'.

- Appearance and achievement of results go together; it is no good doing well if people never look beyond a false image and see the strengths you have

- Communications are perhaps the most important factor influencing how you are seen. You must sound expert, confident and express yourself well in every form of communications from conducting a meeting to writing a report.

5

Your Target Market

Once you have your business up and running you need to decide where your clients are going to come from. With whom do you communicate? The trick here, especially for the smaller operation, is to focus effort on contacting the right people in the right way so as to produce a high strike rate and reduce the necessary quantity of contact that needs to be undertaken to produce the volume of business you want.

First, consider the basics. You need to decide which areas of the river to cast your line into, and, equally important, which to ignore. Considerations here include:

KILLER QUESTIONS

Right, I'm ready to do business: how do I know who my potential clients are?

- *Industry.* Consultants range from those who work for any industry, or for many – right through to some people who only work for one (or for a narrow sector). Sometimes there is an odd mix, dictated by a number of things including experience and potential. For example, I work in many industries, mostly industrial and business to business products and services rather than fast-moving consumer goods, but also have certain sectors where I can offer specialised help – these include work with professional services firms, in publishing and with hotels. The focus here may be an industry one or it may revolve more around particular products.

- *Functional area.* Your work may be specific to specific functions in business: marketing (one of mine), production or IT say.

- *Work area.* Here the focus is on what you do – management training (one of mine), change management and more

- *Level of decision maker.* This is the strike point defining who precisely you must sell to. Bear in mind that often more than one person is involved, but be aware of who they are and who is most important.

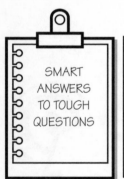

SMART
ANSWERS
TO TOUGH
QUESTIONS

Q: What if I want to work for individuals rather than some kind of organization?

A: The principle is similar. You need to define the market, for instance by age, gender, location, job, life stage, etc. Once you are clear about the kind of people who interest you, then you can move on to think about how to communicate with them. At the stage where your market is simply 'the world and his wife' the task is overpowering, and forming a manageable plan to access them is largely impossible.

Direct or indirect

As well as having a clear focus on who precisely you want as clients, you need to consider the way in which you will access work. You can promote and sell by communicating directly with potential clients or go via other people or organizations. Or both. These 'referral routes' vary in nature. For example, in my own business some leads come via:

- *Writing.* I get enquiries from articles (and books – feel free!) and get paid for writing them too, but I have to try to match the things I do with their potential to produce enquiries. Writing in a magazine aimed at sales and marketing people is well matched to produce leads in that area of work. Some articles may produce nothing, others numbers of enquiries, and it is well nigh impossible to know which will do what. What experience does show is that a regular flow of visible activities in this category do produce regular leads

- *Serving on committees.* This is more time consuming and you are unlikely to get paid, but can be useful. Everyone has got some things like this that they can do – whether in trade, professional or industry bodies – or whatever.

In terms of targeting where you make your first contacts, whether promotional or sales, you need to consider those that will be made direct to potential clients, and others that are a means to an end, in parallel. The appropriate amount of time and effort must be directed at each. Experience helps, of course, and a view of the respective costs may influence your decision too – you may want to spend more time and less money to achieve something; or vice versa.

A market is all the actual or potential buyers of your services. The potential market is those who exhibit specific interest in your kind of service. The qualified market is those who meet the criteria necessary to allow them to become real clients, they have the interest, the need and the funding. A target market is the sub-set of all this upon which you decide to concentrate.

Smart things to say

KILLER QUESTIONS

How can I work out how my market works so that I have a simple, clear and actionable overview?

Leaving actual promotional activity on one side for later chapters, we will turn to how you can actually analyse the complexity that is building up here and decide how best to deploy your activity in its various directions.

It is one thing to have a clear idea of the kind of person you need to be in touch with, but it can also be confusing. You may want to contact chief executives, training or IT managers in large companies, local companies, companies in the Middle East – wherever. But where do you direct the time and how do you proportion your efforts?

Deciding an appropriate focus

Ideas that achieve a lot with no more sophistication than some figuring on the back of an envelope always appeal to me. One such is the idea of *market maps*. Originated to track channels in complex markets, they provide a powerful picture, allowing decisions and action to be taken to focus activity in the right direction.

SMART
PEOPLE
TO HAVE
ON YOUR
SIDE

Michael T. Wilson

To the best of my knowledge the term 'market map' or 'market system map' was originated my Michael T. Wilson in his book *The Management of Marketing* (Gower Publishing); although this was published some time ago (1989 was the last edition) it remains a valuable text. The map aids analysis, planning and implementation, it describes the nature of the system, shows all the channels in existence or use, and can be quantified to show what is happening where.

As a simple example of a map, one showing the various channels involved in the book publishing industry is shown as Figure 5.1 (this is reproduced from the book *Channel Management* published by Capstone Publishing in their Express Exec series).

Paraphrasing the approach advocated by Wilson, preparing a map means:

1. listing the categories of consumer or end-users, and any subdivisions they may contain;

2. listing also any additional influencers (e.g. people having the role that architects do in specifying building materials);

3. asking questions about customers and their characteristics so that information is clear alongside how their purchasing relates to the map, for example:

    — Who are they? (For example, male/female, age, buying power,etc., for individuals and comparable information for industrial buyers – type of industry, etc.).

    — What are their needs? (For example, for value, performance, convenience, etc. – such factors can be linked specifically to a particular product).

    — How are their needs being satisfied? (By both direct and, if relevant, indirect competition)

    — where do they buy? (Linking to the different channels featured on the map.)

This process may necessitate assembling significant amounts of data and ensuring that sales figures can be produced accurately in the right form, even some research may be useful. So be it. The detail is worth assembling and, with the right set-up – e.g. computer programmes that will link conventional sales data into 'channel form' – much of it can be regularly updated very easily. Given the information, and a map to illustrate what is happening, there are several benefits stemming from the approach, it:

* assists planning and setting strategy (which channels to use/not use);

* monitors performance, allowing action to be taken to fine-tune marketing action directed at specific channels;

- highlights the relationships involved (which customers use which channels, etc.);
- allows a view to be taken of matters such as pricing and profitability that reflects what is happening, not in an overall sense, but in the way individual channels work.

It is a concept upon which various tunes can be played, and which can assist in a variety of ways. The following example, shows just one aspect of this, and illustrates how reviewing channels can lead to fundamental changes in marketing approach.

This market map approach can be applied in two ways to consulting. First, as Figure 5.2 shows, to get a quick overview of how your market works. Secondly, it is possible to link such a view to an existing business, put in some figures (even estimates can be useful) and use the analysis to quantify the proportionate value of different routes to fee earning work and different kinds of client.

This is an exercise worth doing and worth making individual; for example categories such as overseas or intermediaries may be split into the various subsections appropriate to you. The categories on the chart can be used, extended or ignored and you can put your own definitions alongside the basic structure that is set out.

Work once removed

Another area that is worth thinking through, listing and prioritizing is any source or method where effort can be applied to prompt incoming enquiries. Some examples, which are not mutually exclusive, include:

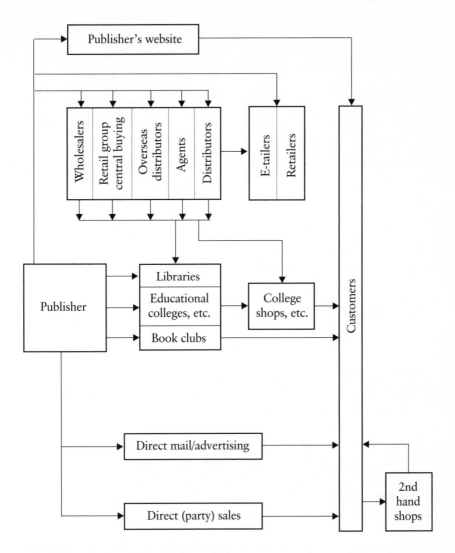

Figure 5.1 Marker map for book publishing

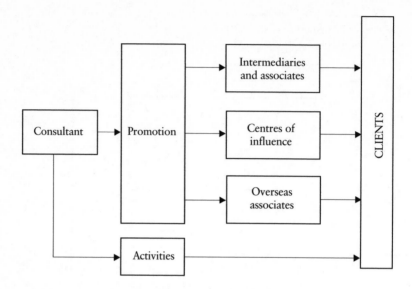

Figure 5.2 Marker map for consultancy

- *'Recommenders'* – any individual who might be able to introduce you to prospective clients. The range here is enormous and is also specific to any individual consultant.

- *Collaborators* – these I define as those you might act jointly with on certain kinds of project, pooling your expertise and enabling you to do things together that neither could do alone. You might find such projects; or they might. You can usefully spend time keeping in touch with such people and finding new possibilities.

- *Centres of influence* – these are bodies that can pass you on to others. They include trade, professional and industry bodies chosen to suit your work focus. They might include chambers of commerce, trade associations and more; some may themselves be clients (or potential clients) others may be such that they can only recommend.

- *Committees* – these have been mentioned and are worth a thought, though you need to ration your time carefully. Do not get locked into one (feeling guilty if you drop out) if it proves unproductive; swap it for another.

- *Public relations activities* – this may embrace action to prompt news items of various sorts (for which you will not be paid) and paid writing assignments that also produce visibility.

- *Networking* – any other miscellaneous contacts that need creating and developing

- *Events* – conferences and exhibitions, indeed any event, at which you can meet and network with people who are potential clients or potentially helpful in some way.

We will return to more about all of these later when promotion is examined in more detail. Here the point to emphasize is that every such area needs examining and pruning – any analysis of the sort recommended in this chapter will produce vastly more potential opportunities than time will allow you to take advantage of. The trick is to select what you do – and do not do – in light of the overall focus you have decided upon for the business. You can always make exceptions, but you must concentrate on the main issues.

There are, of course, other ways of producing work and time will doubtless need to be allowed for prospecting or promotion the exact

Q: I am on a host of committees, belong to and attend the meetings of a variety of bodies, it does produce leads but it is so time consuming – how can I reduce the load?

A: You have to focus or you will never have an evening at home. Keep careful records. There is a difference between something that is interesting or fun to do and something that pays off in business terms. The 80/20 rule doubtless operates. Some of your involvements will produce more than others: concentrate on them and do not keep on with no-hopers that will probably never produce anything. Look at other things you can do as well, maybe one new involvement can replace two or three existing ones. If you work with other people, share out this activity and spread the load (while playing to individuals strengths).

nature of which must, in turn, be tied back to the focus of your business and the kind of work and client you target.

Communication categories

There is a saying about different strokes for different folks. The same sentiment is due in considering clients. Clients, like anyone else, are individuals. As such they need individual attention. You may need to communicate with potential clients in larger groups. However it works in your chosen sector, you need to consider the communications implications. Questions such as: how easy is it to identify and contact people? How often is it worth contacting individuals or groups? What method of contact is best? All these need thinking about.

Incidentally, communications matters are immensely important in actually doing fee-earning work with clients. Some clients, I have one such, never do anything but email, others may want everything in writing (and want it every five minutes). Creating an agreed style of communication and sticking to it – giving people what they want in this way – is vital to good client relationships; and thus to retaining and developing their business.

Q: How can I be sure that my overview of my target market is correct?

A: The simple answer is that this is impossible. Markets are dynamic and things change as you watch. You can be sure of a reasonable match if you think it through and apply common sense and analysis of the facts. Beyond that you need to keep the review up to date. As an example, let me quote a situation I came across with a client of mine (a medium-sized consulting firm in the financial area). I asked what kind of firm constituted a typical client and the MD was able to define this clearly (the details do not matter). I asked what proportion of their clientele this group made up, no exact figure was forthcoming, but it was confidentially said to be 'about two-thirds'. Later, examining the actual figures, it became clear that it was about one-third. The estimate had doubled the reality. What is worse, a whole series of things in the sales and promotional area were being directed at their market as if the estimate was correct. This meant that time and money were wasted and that communications sent, or a significant number of them, were simply not well matched to the actual nature of the recipients.

Such misjudgement is easily made (here the two-thirds represented a situation two to three years back), and an eye must always be kept on trends and change so that no unwarranted assumptions are made.

SMART
ANSWERS
TO TOUGH
QUESTIONS

Finally here, it is worth keeping an eye on every aspect affecting the way people need to be dealt with. For example, I have noticed in recent years that the majority of the prime contacts/decision makers who I have as clients are women; the reverse of the situation in earlier years. They include training or human resources managers, managing directors, marketing people and more. I am not sure what this proves (other than that things change), and I am still trying to decide the communications implications! It may be that part of your targeting should involve thinking about what kinds of person you get on best with, sell to most easily and give you the most cost-effective basis from which to work.

Having a clear target market firmly in mind acts to direct your activities and prevent dissipation of effort. Without this you are in danger of letting events run you and finding that your way of working is not a cost effective one. The tail must not wag the dog.

Now, with target areas for business clearly in mind you can turn to how to communicate with people persuasively, indeed to the whole question of promotion. This is the topic of the next chapter.

6

Promoting Your Business

You are going to need to do some active promotion, the only questions are how much and what form should it take? Let us be clear about the nature of promotion first.

The promotional mix

There are a number of forms of promotion. They are not simple alternatives, they are different in nature and in how they work; and in cost. Figure 6.1 gives an overview.

It shows how different broad methodologies work in different ways – they are distanced differently from the customer, as you go down the chart they

KILLER QUESTIONS

How do I tell the world that I am here and what I do?

Figure 6.1 The promotion mix

become more focused. So certain techniques will work in certain ways. Overall the job is fourfold:

- To select a mix that works effectively; that means primarily one that succeeds in influencing the kind of contacts you want to turn into clients (rather than which is convenient for you – this may be a consideration, but must not outweigh other factors).

- To target appropriately at your chosen market segments, directing messages at both potential clients and at the various intermediaries important to your business.

- To implement an amount of activity across the chosen mix systematically and creatively; not least this means pacing it across the year.

- To co-ordinate activities to minimize effort and maximize results (e.g. you might write an article the content of which forms a conference paper and use a news item about one of them as an inherent part of a mailing; many examples of this sort of crossover can be found).

Internally, perhaps the intention is very clear. You want to spend as little time and money as possible on promotion, ensuring that what you do do has the effect you want. The 'effect you want' may be more than simply producing the desired quantity of fee earning work. You want the right sort of work, at the right time and commanding the right level of fees. You may also have longer-term aims than just producing the work for the next period; perhaps you plan to extend your range of work and are looking for a gradual change in the proportions of the different things you do. You may also have one-off, short-term plans that your promotion must address. For example, I will aim to sell as many copies of this book as possible immediately after publication (the newness and launch never repeat and must be taken advantage of at a precise time).

A *promotional plan*

Before examining the ins and outs of the individual techniques as they might help consulting services, we need to be clear about the context in which they will be used. You need a promotional plan and you need it in writing. This does not need to be elaborate – a year-planning chart and a few notes are often enough. Seeing the plan laid out helps co-ordinate activities. For example, plan a small mailing and the timing of writing and printing a brochure might usefully go on the chart as well as the mailing date; this will help ensure it is actually ready on the due date.

Look at the pattern of the year and of your working. Bear in mind the inherent lead times. You begin to see when it is appropriate to do what.

Consider the pools in which you are aiming to fish. What goes to clients and how often? How do you tap into a particular list or group? Some things are very much a reflection of the calendar. These range from such simple things as the fact that Christmas cards are sent in December and that August is not the best month (in the UK holiday season) for your biggest promotion of the year, to more significant initiatives that you plan.

The plan is a 'rolling' plan. At any given moment it might set out close to a hundred per cent of what you plan to do over the next three months, with a smaller percentage of activity planned for subsequent months. You might want to look at a period of more than a year. Some dates are dictated for you (like the publication of this book), others are a matter of picking the best moments – for the recipients of your promotion and for you.

You may also link your plan to some targets: a press release every month, or so many direct mail shots a week, perhaps. Everything can be adapted in the light of real events – with activities being delayed or

SMART VOICES

Perhaps the most important thing in considering promotion is to divorce it from fee-earning work. Promotional and sales work must be done when its objectives dictate, the ad hoc route of only taking real time to think about promotion when fee-earning work is low is fatal and can only lead to your suffering from some element of the classic feast and famine syndrome. Work plans simply must allow time for promotion, not only to do it, but to choose what is done wisely and implement it well.

Anthony Jacks, marketing consultant and co-author of How to be Better at Marketing (Kogan Page)

beefed up to fit with your intentions and what is going on at a particular event. There is no point in following a plan slavishly, that is not its purpose, it is as much there as a mechanism for organized fine-tuning. For example, in the late spring last year I booked my single largest job ever just ahead of my executing promotional plans linked to the coming summer (traditionally a low time for training). All change, but no problem; and I spent less money than I expected.

With the need for a clear plan of action in mind we can turn to the techniques and how to use them. Not all marketing methods are appropriate. We can rule out a number of things: Tupperware-style tea parties, sponsorship (unless you are of some size) and television advertising for example. The main methods that seem to work for business of this kind are: press and public relations, certain kinds of advertising, direct mail, and a number of promotional mechanisms (from brochures to websites and newsletters). We review something of each in turn.

Public relations

This addresses the area of image and visibility. Public relations acts as the umbrella term for everything of a PR nature and also for that aspect of it that is not better described as press relations. First, consider the overall considerations.

Image

This is important in two ways. To give people who do not know you a feeling for what kind of operation you are, and to describe and explain it to those who do know you, but perhaps have only a superficial picture at this stage. You need to think about such things as:

- *Graphic image* – everything from the look of your office door, reception area and meeting room if you have them, to your letterheads, report covers and business cards. It needs to be smart, modern and professional; more of some of this anon.

- *Telephone answering* – first contact must be organized efficiently, even when you are not there to do it personally (think about how you organize messages: an answerphone, message service, etc.).

- *Other routes to contact* – emails, faxes and so on must all be used appropriately and answered promptly. Small details such as using a signature on your e-mail are a convenience for people (they do not have to look up your address) and can provide an opportunity to say just a little about yourself.

Anything visible, from a Christmas gift to a simple handout, must play its part in creating or enhancing your image. The part played is often quite small but no opportunity should be overlooked. This is not just a matter of internal things, but also of taking advantage of external ones too. For example, get yourself listed in any of the many directories that may allow you a free entry and make sure that any description you use, which must usually be brief, encapsulates your message well.

Press relations

Mentions in the media are well proven as a way of increasing your visibility in a way that produces enquiries. Some of these come through mentions, perhaps via a press release or interview, written by someone other than yourself; others come by doing something editorial – like an article (which you might get paid for), or even a book. If you do not want to do such things, or feel it is beyond your writing skills, then you can consider co-authorship or even using a ghost writer.

Things done in this way are doubly valuable in that copies of items published can be circulated and used in conjunction with other kinds of publicity, thus getting more from the time it takes.

Anything done with the media needs some organizing, almost certainly some persistence and there is no guarantee it will work as you want it to. It is, however, very useful and there is no reason to believe the media will be hostile (is there?) so a good rate of strike is possible. Certainly the opportunities are legion if you include things like regional and local press, technical and industry publications and more.

How to start

Where, then, do you start? Press releases (i.e. notices you send out) can be in the form of routine mentions or more particular stories, but remember that much of the impact of both sorts of material is cumulative. Clients will sometimes comment that '*We seem to see mentions of you pretty regularly*', but have difficulty remembering the exact context of what was said or, more likely, written. To achieve this cumulative impact, you need to be constantly on the lookout for opportunities of gaining a mention.

Dealing with the media is not rocket science. There are ground rules, and conventions. There are tricks of the trade and techniques. It can be learned.

Paul Richards, public relations expert and author of *Be Your Own Spin Doctor* (Take That Ltd)

SMART QUOTES

Even routine matters, perhaps the appointment of a new member of staff or a move of offices, may be written up. All that is necessary is, first, to remember to make these announcements and then to take a disproportionate amount of care and attention as to how they are made. For instance, any announcement that lends itself to a press release is much more likely to be printed if there is a photograph with it. This takes a little more organizing, but is well worth the trouble.

Beyond the routine announcement, matters can get a little more complicated. News means exactly that! While it may be of interest to you that the firm is ten years old, inhabits an eighteenth-century mansion or is reorganizing, a journalist will tend to find it difficult to imagine readers starry-eyed with excitement as they read it in their newspaper or journal. You will have to find something with more of an element of news in it; it may be genuinely different, it may be a first comment on something, but it must truly have something of real interest about it.

If you become known as a source of good comment, stories and articles, then your press contacts will start to come to you and the whole process may gain continuity and momentum. There is, after all, a world of journalists, editors and others with deadlines to meet, space to fill – and they are often worried about how to do it week after week, or month after month. So too are those in other media such as local radio (incidentally, if you are asked to appear on radio, get a little advice – it is very different to other media, not least in the lack of length at which you can speak). They will certainly respond to some of the ideas that come to them.

So, public relations is an area that can go beyond simply producing awareness of your operation. It can also paint a particular picture of it – creating not just understanding, but a positive interest in your firm that

Q: How do I give my press release the best chance of successfully prompting a mention?

A: Apart from making sure that what it describes is 'news', press releases demand that certain conventions are complied with; at least editors will pay more attention to them if they do. This is spelt out in the checklist below. You should not follow this slavishly: remember that an element of creativity is always necessary.

Composing a press release

There are two, perhaps conflicting, aspects of putting together a press release that will stand a good chance of publication. The first is to comply with the 'form' demanded by the newspapers, magazines and journals to whom you send your release; the second is to stand out as being of genuine interest from the very large number of releases received. We will take the 'form' first.

SMART
ANSWERS
TO TOUGH
QUESTIONS

- It should carry the words 'Press (or News) Release' at the top, together with the date, preferably at the top left-hand side of the first page.

- If an embargo is necessary (i.e. a request not to publish before a certain date, to ensure any news items appear as near as possible simultaneously – as once an item has been in print others will consider it of less interest), then it should be clearly stated 'EMBARGO: not to be published before (time) on (date)'. Use capitals for emphasis.

- Also, at the top you need a heading, not too long but long enough to indicate clearly the contents of the release or to generate interest in it.

- Space it out well with wide margins, reasonable gaps between paragraphs and so on. This allows sub-editors to make notes on it.

- If it runs to more than one page, make sure it says 'continued' or similar at the foot of the page, even breaking a sentence at the end of the page will make it more likely people will turn over.

- Similarly, to make it absolutely clear that there is no more, many people put 'end' at the foot of the last page.

- Use newspaper style. Short paragraphs. Short sentences. Two short words rather than one long one.

- Keep it brief, long enough to put over the message and on to a second page if necessary, but no more.

- The first sentences are crucial and need to summarize as far as possible the total message.
- Avoid overt 'plugging' (although that may well be what you are doing). Do not mention names, for example, right at the beginning, for example.
- Try to stick to facts rather than opinions: a financial consultant saying '. . . this event is being arranged for all those who are interested in minimizing their tax liability', for example, is better than '. . . this event will be of great interest to all those wanting to minimize their tax liability'.
- Opinions can be given, in quotes and ascribed as such to an individual. This works well and can be linked to the attachment of a photograph (which should usually be a black and white print and clearly labelled in case it gets separated from the release, coupled perhaps with the offer to send an electronic version of it).
- Do not overdo the use of adjectives, which can jeopardize credibility.
- Avoid underlining things in the text (underlining is used as an instruction to printers to italicize the text).
- Separate notes to the journal from the text as footnotes, for example, 'photographers will be welcome'; they could get printed as part of the story.
- Never omit from a release, at the end, a clear indication of from whom further information can be sought and their telephone number (even if this is on the heading of the first page).
- Make sure finally that it is neat, well typed and presentable and that it lists enclosures. It may be obvious perhaps, but important.

So, how do you make your press release stand out? There are fewer rules here, but two points are certainly worth bearing in mind.

- Do not 'cry wolf'. Save releases for when you really have a story. If you send a series of contrived releases, there is a danger that a good one among them will be ignored.
- Make sure the story sounds interesting and without overdoing things, be enthusiastic about it. If you are not, why would they be? Perhaps the only good thing in the world that is contagious is enthusiasm.

whets people's appetite for more information, prompts enquiries, re-establishes dormant contacts and reinforces your image with existing clients.

Not only is public relations activity potentially a powerful weapon in your promotional armoury, it is also free. Well, it seems free when compared with advertising, which is communication in bought space, but there is a catch. It takes time! And in any small, fee-earning business, time is certainly money. Therefore, too often, public relations is neglected because people are busy, even over-stretched, and opportunities are missed. Yet if the power of public relations is consistently ignored, then at worst not only are opportunities missed, but the image that occurs by default may actually damage business prospects.

In many ways, therefore, time spent on public relations is time well spent. It is an area in which you should leave no stone unturned, since many things can have a PR effect and some of the more personal ones give rise to sales opportunities. Consider whether you can find openings to:

- Speak at a conference or event of some kind.

- Write an article, column or other feature for some publication.

- Judge a competition (there are many events for small business, often locally organized).

- Belong to something where you will meet the right people (a trade or professional body, maybe).

- Sponsor something/someone.

- Sit on or chair a committee.

Some of those above are aspects of networking to which we return later. Do not reject such things out of hand. There are many consultants using such methods and gaining advantage from them.

The trouble with opportunities is that they so often come disguised – as hard work.

Anon., quoted in *Hook Your audience* (Management Pocketbooks)

All it takes is time, effort (and confidence) to set them up. You will not succeed with everything like this you try, indeed you will not succeed first time with many of your efforts; but some will work, and anything that allows you to demonstrate your competence is the best advertisement of all. The first step is to be observant and spot opportunities: press relations (like most promotion) is in part a state of mind.

While you cannot rely on public or press relations for the total promotional job that is necessary, it can and should provide a sound foundation for promotion. It is specifically suitable when budgets are low and can work effectively in tandem with other techniques to create the right overall impact.

Advertising

Advertising is not usually a good way to promote a small consultancy business. It is expensive and what is done must be creatively presented, and appear often enough and large enough to have impact. However, there are exceptions. These are almost all specialist, in terms of both media and message. For example, one of the areas in which I work is with professional service firms, a very specific pool of potential clients. A regular advertisement in the journal *Professional Marketing*, which is focused solely on marketing in that sector, does create exposure and produce leads. Such industry-focused ideas may be worth seeking out.

Think very carefully before undertaking very much of this sort, however; and a particular caution: do not go unthinkingly into advertising supplements and features in your chosen area just because they are there – make sure they meet your specific objectives.

Direct mail

This is a technique that works well for consultants.

Direct mail has a mixed reputation, yet only the worst of it should be called 'junk mail'. Although some perhaps deserves that description, the best does not, or it would not be used and would not work.

Nevertheless, despite its prevalence and usefulness, somehow feelings about direct mail sometimes seem to run high. Some people regard it as

SMART
ANSWERS
TO TOUGH
QUESTIONS

Q: Must I post direct mail, what about fax and email?

A: You might put a brochure into a journal of some sort as an insert; this can work well. Otherwise, one class of mail decidedly worthy of the name junk mail is that increasing number of communications that nowadays arrive by fax, and more recently by email. When sent cold, these are totally self-defeating, they tie up people's phone lines, use their paper and cost them money. Most people seem to resent them deeply and their use is not recommended. So the answer is simply – no.

intrusive. Everyone appears to know someone who has been mailed three times in the same week about something entirely inappropriate, and addressed wrongly as 'Dear Madam'.

Direct mail is, though, only a form of advertising. No more, no less; albeit a specialized form. It is used very successfully in a wide range of industries and applications, many of them perfectly respectable – charities, banks, building societies and so on. Many others are dependent on it as their main form of promotion or because it results in a major proportion of their sales (indeed, one example of this is business books like this one.) What is more, although of course there is the occasional annoyance, it is used for the most part without upsetting the people to whom it is directed. Indeed, some will even pay to receive it. I pay to receive mailings from the Barbican, and other examples are various catalogues; one I like is *The Good Book Guide*. If people are not interested, they throw direct mail material away, a process that is not really so unlike turning over an advertisement page in a magazine in which one is not interested. Of course direct mail is wasteful. It hurts to think of so many carefully penned words ending up in the bin (at least it hurts the originator!). But it is no more wasteful than other forms of advertising. All advertising is in a sense wasteful – what matters is whether it produces a cost-effective response, whether it pays for itself long term.

Contrary to some popular belief, direct mail is nearly always opened and much of it is read. In the UK, the Post Office, which spends a great deal of time and money studying the effectiveness of direct mail, recently demonstrated through research that more than 90 per cent of it is opened and more than 75 per cent of it is read. The trick for users is less to achieve this, therefore, than to ensure an offering will stand out from others, will generate interest and will be seen as persuasive.

The nature of direct mail

Direct mail is not an alternative to advertising, rather it adds to the range of techniques available. It is no more a magic formula than any other individual technique. But it can sometimes suit well. It is flexible; certainly more flexible than advertising. Direct mail may mean either four letters, or 40, 400, 4,000 or 40,000. It does not have to be done on the grand scale, it can be targeted at small, specific groups; it can be undertaken progressively with so many shots per week or month being sent – useful for small companies. It is personal and can be directed at specific and discrete groups – not just engineering companies, say, but the production managers of agricultural engineering companies in East Anglia, for instance. It is controllable, it can be tested, implemented progressively and results can be monitored to ensure it provides a cost-effective element in the total promotional mix. As it is likely to be low cost per contact, and campaigns can be varied so much in size, there are few consultants who could not usefully experiment with the technique. It can be specific or it may be directed broadly, selling the firm, or be part of the promotion of particular aspect of your services.

Direct mail can aim to do numbers of things, for example:

- Prompt an order (fill in the form, send a cheque and something is then delivered).

- Prompt requests for more information: brochures, etc.

- Arrange an appointment and set up a meeting.

- Encourage clients to visit something like an exhibition where they can meet you and move on to other stages.

- Link to demonstrations, samples, visits and more. It is as important in the multi-stage process involved in selling consultancy, to move the process to another stage, as it is in situations where stimulating an order is the immediate intention.

So, direct mail has a lot going for it. It is a proven technique in many fields. It can be used on a small scale, it can be targeted on specific market segments, and it can be tested and monitored much more easily than many other forms of promotion. But, it is also deceptive and can appear easier to use than, in fact, it is.

The elements of direct mail

Every element of it needs careful consideration. Among the components are:

- *The list.* Any mailing is only as good as the list of names it is mailed to. It must be appropriate, up to date and personal. Mailings addressed to an individual do best. In many businesses existing customers are as important as prospects, and complex overlapping campaigns are constructed; there is a specialized area of 'data-base marketing' and, though list holding and use is now covered by the Data Protection Act in the UK, sources of lists are valuable. Next time you are asked in a store to write your name and address on the back of the cheque, that may be one of the reasons. Other techniques, such as satisfaction cards, are specifically designed as list builders.

- *The message.* This is vital. Copywriting in this area is a specialist job. Just one phrase changed can increase (or decrease) the response.

There are about three seconds, when something is pulled out of an envelope, during which the recipient decides whether or not to read on further, so immediate impact is crucial.

- *The envelope.* This is part of the message, many are overprinted, perhaps with a 'teaser' message, often a question; what is on them affects response. It is particularly important is assisting the job of getting the recipient to decide to read on, and to do so in the right frame of mind.

- *The letter.* This is vital and is often not short. A good message is as long as is necessary to present an argument to take action and if this takes two or three pages so be it; many letters are longer and work well. As a general rule, a brochure of some sort plus a letter pulls better than a brochure on its own.

- *Brochures.* These provide supporting information in a profusion of ways. They may be coloured, illustrated and, in extreme cases, incorporate a range of gimmicks (in so far as they are compatible with consulting)

Direct mail is a technique where tiny details matter. For instance, a letter with a PS at the end may do better than one without; a reply card with an actual postage stamp (rather than with prepaid postage) may get up to 50 per cent more replies; and certain so called 'magic' words (new, free, guaranteed, exciting) seem to boost response, provided they are not overused. Shots may sometimes be advantageously organized as a double hit. One letter being designed to follow another after a predetermined gap. Such detail is beyond the scope of this chapter. (If the details are important to you, there is a good chapter on the subject in my book *Marketing on a Tight Budget* [Kogan Page] – I justify this mention on the basis that it illustrates seeing opportunities to promote yourself everywhere, sorry I digress.)

Drayton Bird

Advertising man Drayton Bird is an acknowledged expert on direct mail. His book *Commonsense Direct Mail* is, for me, the ultimate bible. It is practical, well illustrated and brings the whole process to life in a way that is easy to read – and easy to draw lessons from. In terms of the way it addresses its topic it is, I think, one of the best business books ever written; certainly it is the best on its subject. He also wrote *How to Write Sales Letters that Sell* which is also excellent (both are published by Kogan Page). Neither address consultancy specifically, indeed they use all sorts of examples, but that does not detract from their usefulness. I wish I had written them.

One more thing: the copy – all the text, i.e. whether in a letter or brochure(s), may not be read in sequence, or at a sitting. People dip in and out of the material, thus some repetition of content between, say, letters and brochures (though perhaps not actual words) may be sensible. Certainly the relationship between what is said in different elements of the shot needs careful consideration.

Promotion

A number of other things may also help your promotional effort. The first two link quite closely with direct mail, and are thus dealt with briefly.

Brochures

A variety of brochures may be used. These may be very simple (a folded A4 sheet, or less) or more elaborate (an A4 folder containing a number of items). Any brochure should be well tailored to:

- The objectives you have for it in terms of results.

- Suit its target audience (prospects, prospects in a certain industry, intermediaries, etc.).

- The way in which it will be used (something to be predominantly mailed may need to be different from something left with people after a meeting).

Design must be smart and modern, but this is easier to achieve than writing what goes inside; back to direct mail principles.

Q: What quantity of brochures do I print?

A: This may be no problem. If the brochure is for a particular mailing, then the list (and some spares) dictates the print run. For general use it can be difficult to estimate numbers, however, and this does need a little thought. Do not, however, let the economies of scale rule out other considerations. The most important question is 'How long will this information be current?' You will want to change things sooner than you think, and using up old, now inappropriate, brochures rather than waste them is not likely to maximize promotional results.

Newsletters

A variety of things are possible here. Newsletters can be particularly useful to create a flow of communication. There is a commitment here that needs to be born in mind: do not announce, say, a quarterly newsletter unless you are really sure that you can sustain your chosen frequency. Newsletters can quickly become lacklustre if ideas tail off and promotion is either useful or just so much wasted money. (Remember the old saying that a woman cannot be half pregnant; it is the same principle.)

Promotional events

Nothing gives you a better opportunity to impress and find new prospects than actually being able to demonstrate your professional competence in some way. Hence promotional events can be a valuable part of your promotional armoury. You can plan and run your own or you can do them in partnership with others. Alternatively, contrive to be an outside speaker on someone else's – I have just attended an accountant's budget 'do' at which several other people took the platform; it made for a better event for all and was well worth doing as the 'junior partners' were given good visibility.

However you do them they must be good, and therefore well thought out. A poor venue, handouts or presentation will impress no one. Every detail must be right; I have long remembered an event at which after a video had been shown in a hotel conference room no one could find the light switch and the poor (unprepared) organizer was reduced for fumbling round the walls for what seemed like forever.

So you need to do the following:

1. *To plan thoroughly* The thoroughness with which this is done pays dividends. No stone unturned, no opportunities missed. The starting point is to set clear objectives. Why this event? Why in this form? Why at this time? Why these particular people invited? What should they get from it? Such thinking should incorporate a broad view: for example making sure that the event fits into your overall promotional strategy (and budget) to create the right mix.

If there is more than one of you, put someone in charge; this can be a classic too-many-cooks area. If you want a theme around which to hang the organizing of the event, then the simplest and most pertinent approach is to fix on what attendees will get *from* it. If they will:

- Hear or see something useful

- Receive valuable handouts

- Like and enjoy the location or venue

- Meet others who may interest or be useful to them

yet not find it too time-consuming, then they are more likely to respond positively to an invitation and, on attending, believe that they have done the right thing. Everything about the event must be organized to support such a view.

2. *Invitations*   No event can be regarded as successful unless it attracts the right people. You may want to invite clients or prospects; or both. Indeed a mix is often regarded as best. If the clients are contented clients they will help sell to the others. In addition, there may be a range of intermediaries and recommenders that warrant a place. Any invitation must be attractive. It must not be a simple introspective plug, but paint a picture of something organized to be genuinely interesting and valuable.

A simple invitation may not be sufficient. A mix of promotional activity may be necessary. For example, a press release might be used to announce certain events, mention might also be made of it in a newsletter, or an article based on something to be presented at the event might be placed in a suitable journal (a productive use of the time taken in preparation). Thus, an overlapping series of actions might be arranged to back up the issuing of the invitation and maximize the response. More individual action might also be arranged – for example individual telephone calls could be made, designed to convert interest in someone who has seen other promotion into confirmation of attendance.

Thoroughness is necessary throughout this process, A checklist or calendar chart may be useful to keep track of everything. Details, such as the copy – a truly promotional what's in it for you explanation – are important. So too are the decisions made about such things as venue and all those aspects that will be part of the overall impression that people will take away. A truly businesslike and suitable venue (assuming your offices do not offer this) may make all the difference to the atmosphere and how things go. Conversely an ill-judged decision to give participants, say, a tacky ballpoint pen may niggle and dilute the good impression given.

3. *Briefing*   You must brief carefully; the difference between confusion and excellence on the day may be directly down to this. So brief:

- *The presenters* – if there is more than yourself, and particularly if some are from outside your own organization (similarly, follow your briefing if you appear at others' events – for example, respect for time is vital and if you overrun your slot and disrupt the timetable you are unlikely to be top of their list to ask again).

- *Support staff* – any administrative or secretarial staff must understand their role exactly.

- *The venue* – there must be no misunderstandings. If whoever is in the chair says 'Let's pause for coffee', then it must be absolutely certain that it will be ready, hot and waiting as the door opens. Again this is an area of details. You may need to consider display space, equipment (anything used – microphone, projector, etc. – should be checked to make sure it works as you want; do not take the venue's word for it), signs (you do not want people unable to find the meeting room), lights, heating – everything. Even lacklustre biscuits at the break can have people muttering 'cheapskate' and dilute the overall impression.

4. *The message* However well things are organized, above all what people have come to hear must be good. This means that topics must be well chosen, sufficient detail given: not so little as to fail to inform or generate interest, without going on and on (or precluding the need for your services because you have told people everything they need to know!). It also means that what is said must be well presented. This is another issue, beyond our brief here, but it must achieve positive impact. This means care in preparation, perhaps even practice and rehearsal. The effort is worthwhile. If someone knows their stuff, and it shows, if the audience identifies with what is said and how something is handled, the effect is powerful. It gets the audience thinking along exactly the lines you want: that's a good point . . . I hadn't thought of it like that before . . . this is something I should watch.

5. *Follow up* Finally, events need following up. Some people may come up at the end and request a meeting; others may need prompting. But that is surely the whole purpose: talk to the group – subsequently talk to some people individually – and later have them as new (and repeating?) clients. Always take follow action promptly, especially when you are fulfilling requests to renew contact.

This is an area well worth investigating, whether you set things up yourself or simply seek opportunities to link with others, almost nothing acts more certainly as effective promotion than you literally demonstrating your professional expertise.

Basic documentation

Whatever mix of promotional methods you may use, you always need a number of things, all a fundamental part of your promotional armoury:

Binder

You will need a professional-looking way of presenting longer documents including proposals and reports. You may consider it is worth having your own binding machine – choose something that allows documents to lay flat when open – and certainly you need smart covers (perhaps a colour that matches your letterhead). Some businesses may need something more elaborate, as with a ring binder for training course notes.

Biographical notes

People will often want to know something of your background and experience. The document that is required here is not the conventional CV, or a chronological list of jobs done. It must blend evidence of experience, activities and achievements. It may include things as varied as a project for an individual client to a position on a committee.

There is one overriding rule here: *there is no such thing as a standard document for this.*

By all means have standard material stored on computer; indeed do not only keep it, but update it regularly. But not only must you have several versions of it, but whichever you choose as an appropriate basis for a particular purpose or client *must be amended every time.* The emphasis must be right. You may want a focus that is right to send when aiming to work:

Daniel Foo

Daniel Foo, a manager with FMC Southeast Asia Pte Ltd in Singapore, has a clever idea for his business card (he is not a consultant, so if you steal this idea you are taking it into a new area).

His card is printed on a shaped card, a shape that we are all familiar with from examples of optical illusions. Put two cards down one above the other and one seems clearly larger (see below); in fact they are identical. Of no significance other than as a bit of fun, but memorable.

Tony Teo

Tony Teo is a property consultant working in Southeast Asia. His business card has the words CALL ME on the front and nothing else but his photograph and telephone number. On the reverse of a card that is a tiny 6 cm × 4 cm (half the size of many 'standard' cards) it says:

THE LACK OF BUSINESS FROM YOU
HAS MADE THIS ECONOMY-SIZED
CARD NECESSARY

Below that are his other contact details. Is this too much of a gimmick? Maybe: it would not suit everyone — but Tony has a regular card too so can choose when and when not to use this special one. Whatever else, it is memorable.

- In a specific industry

- In a particular country overseas

- In a certain size of organization

- On a particular kind of project

The additional time taken to achieve this is always worthwhile. Be selective. You cannot include everything and may need to select a certain length as suitable (one page, say), or to follow a brief.

Factsheets

Brochures are mentioned elsewhere. By factsheets is meant the kind of thing that might be produced as A4 sheets, and perhaps included as appendices in proposals. These might highlight particular individual services you provide, those directed at a specific industry or designed to highlight any other aspect of your business offering that you may want to draw attention to separately from a more general statement. As an example of an individual one, I use a list of published books and 'flyers' about individual titles.

Letterheads and business cards

These have already been mentioned, in discussing image, and need to be good – they will get a great deal of use and need to work hard for you.

Websites

We live in a dynamic world and technology has a way of creeping up on you. One day the internet is an uncertain prediction, now we are all learning to surf and references to e-commerce are all around. You may have bought this book by contacting a website (the publishers Capstone have one which is: www.capstoneideas.com), and many businesses of all sorts, even small ones, have their own website. Indeed to create something simple is now a classic low-cost option.

It is not my purpose here to explain the technology, indeed I am hardly qualified to do so. However, a website is no more than a new option in the promotional mix and needs to be considered accordingly. Setting up a website can be time-consuming and expensive; so too can the process of maintaining it and keeping it up to date. Some businesses acted very early as technology created this opportunity. Some acted solely because it was 'something that had to be done', and perhaps to keep up with others, perhaps to pander to the ego of someone involved and enthusiastic. Whatever the reason it was sometimes ill considered and time and money were spent to no good effect. Whatever might be done needs thinking through; if a website can help build your consulting business, then the first question is very obvious and straightforward: *what objectives do you have for your website?*

There may be several, but they should all be specific. It is important to know whether the cost of setting up will deliver what you intend; important, not least, to how the site is developed. Perhaps you aim for the site to be, in part, a source of reference. You want people to consult it to obtain information (and be impressed by it at the same time). This may save them (and you?) time and effort otherwise expended in other ways. Perhaps you intend that it plays a more integral part in the selling process, and you want to measure its effectiveness in terms of counting the number of new contacts it produces and, in turn, how many of those are turned into actual revenue-producing clients.

So, if you already have a website, check whether you have good feedback on its use and the specific results it brings you (e.g. counting new contacts or revenue coming from new clients). Similarly, if you are in the process of setting up a site, ensure that consideration of this is an inherent part of the process.

In addition, you may have products you want people to order and pay for through direct contact with the site. A consultant might offer a survey of some sort, primarily to put an example of their expertise and style in the hands of prospective clients (though it might also be a source of revenue also). In this case not only must the ordering system work well, and this means it must be quick and easier for whoever is doing the ordering, but the follow up must be good too. Any initial good impression given will quickly evaporate if whatever is ordered takes forever to arrive or needs several chasers. One hazard to good service is to demand too much information as an order is placed. Of course, this kind of contact represents an opportunity to create a useful database; but turning ordering into the Spanish Inquisition will hardly endear you to people.

Whatever objectives are decided upon, there are then three distinct tasks. They are to:

- *Attract people to the site*. Just having the site set up does not mean people will log onto it in droves, much less that the people you want to do so will act in this way. Other aspects of promotion must draw attention to it and this may vary from simply having the website address on your letterhead to such things as incorporating mention (and perhaps demonstration) of it into client events.

- *Impress people when they see it* – both with its content and its presentation. This means keeping a close eye on the users' view and the practicalities as it is set up. For example, all sorts of impressive graphics and pictures are possible and can look creative and may well impress. Certainly you will need some. But such devices can take a long time to download, and if that is what you are encouraging people to do they may find this tedious, especially if the graphics seem more like window dressing than something that enhances the content in a way that helps them.

- *Encourage repeat use.* This may or may not be one of the objectives. If it is, then efforts have to be made to encourage recontacting and this too may involve an overlap with other forms of communication.

Beyond this you also need to consider carefully:

- What the content should be (this is an ongoing job, not a one off).

- How the contacting of the website can prompt a dialogue.

- How topical it should be (this affects how regularly it needs revision).

- Its convenience and accessibility (does it have a suitable navigation mechanism?).

- Will it look consistent (and not as if it has been put together by committee).

- The protection it needs (is anything confidential, is it vulnerable to hackers, etc.?).

Overall, it will need the same planning, co-ordination and careful execution as any other form of marketing communication. In addition, it is likely to necessitate active, ongoing co-operation from numbers of people around the firm who will provide and update information. Given how difficult it can be to get even a small group of people to agree on, say, one page of copy for a new brochure, this may present quite a challenge. Clearly responsibility for the site and what it contains must unequivocally laid at someone's door, together with the appropriate authority to see it through (for a sole practitioner the problem all lies at your door).

In addition, someone needs to have the knowledge that is necessary from a technical standpoint. This may be internal or external, but it needs to be linked to an understanding of marketing and/or the ability to accept a clear brief. This is not a case of applying all the available technology, building in every bell and whistle simply because it is possible. Practical solutions are necessary to meet clear objectives.

If a site is to be useful, that is an effective part of the marketing mix, then sufficient time and effort must be put in to get it right. And the ongoing job of maintaining it must be born in mind from the beginning.

A link with research

An interesting and practical development is the availability of standard, cost-effective software packages that can work as an integral part of a website and monitor how it used. In fact, there are now such add-ons better described as research tools. These can not only allow regular research and formal monthly analysis about exactly who is using a website, their precise characteristics, and how and why they are in touch with the site, but also allow the way the system works to be simply tailored to the needs and intentions of an individual firm. The intention is specifically to obtain information that will make the website a more accurate and effective marketing tool.

SMART
ANSWERS
TO TOUGH
QUESTIONS

Similarly, other technological possibilities come along in increasing profusion. For example, it is possible for someone logged onto a website to trigger a phone call from a supplier. Thus you could organize to be able to talk to a potential client as they look at your site or afterwards (they may have only one telephone line). This sort of thing may present logistical problems, but you need to keep up with what is possible as your website users will make comparisons.

Ultimately whether you have a site and how elaborate it is remains a matter of choice (not only about this, but about the overall mix). Some consultants have quite elaborate ones and swear they are invaluable. Others have something simple or nothing at all, and find this suits their overall method of operation.

Networking

Most consultants quote this as perhaps the most important thing to do in order to secure business. Again this has been touched on in various ways elsewhere in the book. Key points are to:

- Assess – systematically – who you should be in touch with.

- Categorize your contact records: using major categories such as potential clients and intermediaries and also collaborators and sub-contractors and those in positions to recommend or introduce you in any way.

- Keep in touch – regularly. Think about the frequency; it needs to be sufficiently often to keep you in peoples' memory, yet not become a nuisance.

- Vary the method – meet people, telephone them, email, send them something – this rings the changes, reduces the likelihood of over-doing it and enhances the likelihood of action resulting

- Be persistent – you may want something to come from a contact at once. This may simply be unrealistic. Keep in touch, remembering that even a year or two of such contact does not take too long or cost very much, and you extend the odds of something good coming of it.

Ruth Webber

Ruth is a marketing consultant, based in Scotland and specializing in the sector of work for professional services firms. The following comment is true in any sector and one that everyone should remember and can use.

'Never be afraid of asking existing clients for introductions to their peers and business acquaintances. They will probably not think to volunteer them, but, if asked, will be happy to oblige.'

To which I would add only to ask carefully but without apology and to use this to ferret out other names around large organizations as much as to obtain a lead into other organizations.

Overall you have to prioritize in this area. You cannot sit on every conceivable committee, have lunch with someone every day and you need to fit everything you do in with normal working life. But do not underestimate it, in conjunction with your promotion and sales activity, this is simply vital.

Remember too that all this overlaps with other personal contacts, especially those described at the end of Chapter 7 designed to follow things through and maintain contact as an extension of the sales process.

Summary

To sum up, perhaps the best way to view promotion is as you would any client assignment or project. You need clear objectives, you need a plan – an action plan – and you need to work systematically and focus your efforts on what works best and pace activity throughout over the months, co-ordinating what you do to get the best from it. Neglect your promotion and you neglect your business. Remember, however, that promotion can usually only produce interest and enquiries. These have to be converted into firm assignments and doing that means deploying personal sales skills; it is to those we turn in the next chapter.

7

Personal and Professional Selling

Now we turn to a key personal skill, that of being persuasive in face-to-face meetings (though the principles here can usefully affect many things from a telephone call to a written communication, a topic picked up in the next chapter). Saying that this is key is in danger of understating things, perhaps it is more true to say that *if you cannot sell, you cannot consult.* Further, it is not just a skill you must develop, but one that must be deployed productively, because unless you achieve a good success rate (booking a good proportion of the leads and situations that you pursue) it will affect your profitability. After all, while you are selling you are not earning – well, not usually.

Before getting into the detail of how to go about the process, four over-riding factors are important to note.

- *Persuasive communication – selling (professional selling) has a complex job to do: it must inform, persuade and differentiate.* While nothing about selling is itself intellectually taxing, and much of what makes it work is common sense, it needs careful orchestrating and any complexity is created by the fact that many aspects of the process need deploying accurately and in parallel.

- *Selling is inherently fragile.* By this I mean that it is sensitive to small change; something done a little differently can make the difference between agreement or rejection. Even a poor choice of a few key words of description can affect the outcome. The details very much matter.

- *Selling must be acceptable to the client.* There is a fear among some consultants that too strong ('pushy') an approach is incompatible with projecting a professional image, and indeed it could be so. Well considered sales approaches, however, can help create, retain, and even enhance, the professional relationship that you are at pains to work within

- *Selling must be deployed in a tailored manner.* There are certainly principles to be borne in mind, but there is no one right way to sell. We can all spend a lifetime learning to adapt better and better to changing conditions and, not least, client demands and expectations. What is necessary is to sell in the best way – whatever that is; on every occasion, meeting by meeting, client by client, approaches must be well matched to the circumstances. Selling consultancy services is no place for a rigid or 'scripted' approach.

Selling in context

As has been said, marketing should pervade all aspects of the business. Attitudes to what services are offered (and not offered), what fees are charged and so on are inherent to the marketing process. But the promotional techniques are the most visible, and are certainly a major element of marketing. No matter how well executed and how creative, they will still, if successful, not produce any new clients of themselves. What they will pro-

> **SMART QUOTES**
>
> Success doesn't come to you, you go to it.
>
> Marva Calins

duce, if successful, is prospects – those sufficiently interested to say *'Tell me more'*. The only thing that can convert that interest into agreement that will produce fees is personal persuasive skills.

Such skills cannot be limited to the most senior people in a firm, still less to only a few of them; they must be spread reasonably widely throughout the firm. Potentially everyone has a role to play. And for the sole practitioner there is no question – they must be able to sell, and sell well. It is not an option; it is a necessity – if they do not do it no one will.

It is this final, and personal, part of the marketing process that this chapter reviews. Success is to an extent in the details, so the process will be dissected and how each element helps the whole examined. It may appear to start with the basics. Indeed it does; but bear in mind the word 'fragile' used earlier, you need to understand the detail to deploy the techniques appropriately and to make them successful. And to do so every time.

Certain points which appear in this chapter are designed to illustrate key points at which what is being done can be made more persuasive, more likely to *differentiate* you from competition. Also, to show how greater persuasiveness can be positioned so that it adds improved client awareness and service, from the prospect's point of view (rather than being seen as 'pushy').

As there are a number of elements to be dealt with in this chapter, we will start by reviewing the nature of the sales process, then turn to the face-to-face situation and then to follow-up activity and other communication techniques.

Fundamentals of success

Whatever kind of consultant you are, clients buy your 'professional competence'. Whatever they want done, from a straightforward project (are any entirely straightforward?) to a complex ongoing involvement, they want to be sure they are dealing with the right firm and the right people. And they will define doing so as working with the one with whom there is the greatest certainty of getting the job done right.

KILLER QUESTIONS

How does a potential client know that working with me will be successful?

Put yourself in the client's shoes for a moment. How do they know a good job will be done? In many ways the answer, if they have not used you or your firm before (and to a degree if they have), is simple. They cannot know. As has been said, intangible services cannot, by definition, be tested.

So, they seek a degree of measurement – prediction – from everything they *can* test. Among the things that contribute to this, the people rank high. Without doubt they will check out the people and, almost always these days, do this alongside checking one, two or more other firms or individuals.

Of course, you and your colleagues are good with people, you are professionally competent and, what is more, you are nice people to do business with. Surely if you create the right relationship their business will follow? Well, perhaps. However, is it just possible that the other firms being checked out have some pleasant and efficient people too? Some people will no doubt do business with you simply because they like you best. The majority, while getting on with consultants they use may be important to them, will also weigh other things in the balance. They want you to be knowledgeable, efficient, reliable; they may want you to have expert knowledge of particular things; they certainly want to feel you understand them, their business and their situation and to act with that understanding in mind. In addition, if they get on with you as well, then so much the better.

Now you and any other people in your firm may be exceptional, able to do the best job possible for a wide range of clients, but, as has been said, the client has to be persuaded of this fact. It follows, as night follows day, that the first chance (and perhaps the only chance) you will have of demonstrating your professional competence is when you are selling. Your excellence may shine through instantly when you start work, but unless it does so earlier, you may never start.

This fact, and the fragile nature of the sales process, both referred to earlier, make it paramount that every element of persuasive communication – professional selling – is done correctly, with 'done correctly' meaning done in away that will maximize the chances of people doing business with you.

A further point is worth adding to this explanation of why selling is so important, and that is productivity – sales productivity, that is. People in consulting firms are expensive (ask any client!). The opportunity cost of everything you do, other than doing or managing fee-earning projects, is considerable. If things are being done inadequately, two meetings where one should have sufficed, or if the success rate of new clients in relationship to the number of prospects with whom you are in discussion is too low, then it becomes a disproportionately expensive process. In a fee-earning business the time taken for selling must be kept low.

The flow chart shown in Figure 7.1 shows the entire process of obtaining business, starting from planning and marketing activity through to individual contact with prospects and on, assuming success, to the client development which should always parallel and run beyond doing the work.

A number of things are clear from this picture. Selling is:

- A *sequential* and *staged* process. Occasionally one meeting may lead directly to business; more often a number of different interactions are necessary, building up the case and finally converting the interest generated into commitment.

- A *cumulative* process. In other words, each stage has to go right, the prospect can lose interest or drop out at any stage and at every stage they may well be making comparisons with how a competing firm goes through the process. Literally, if one stage is judged inadequate by the prospect, there may well be no chance to move on to the next stage at all.

- The stages clearly involve different *methods of communication*, all of which must be handled with equal effectiveness. What is done must

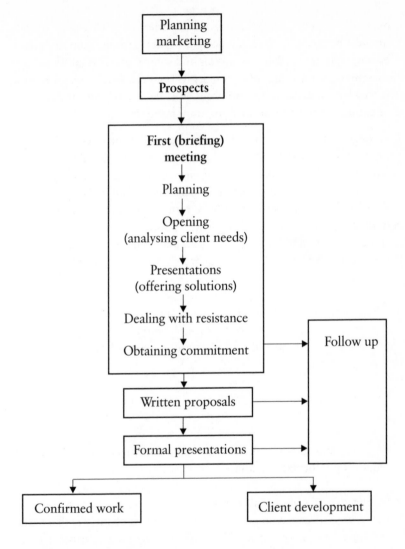

Figure 7.1 The process of obtaining business

be equally persuasive, no matter whether it involves a simple one-to-one meeting, a telephone call, written communication (letters or longer, more complex proposals and so on), or a formal 'stand-up' presentation. Each method presents its own challenges, may demand somewhat different skills and none must be a weak link in the chain of communication resulting in definite business.

To a degree this means that selling is a complex process. Remember none of the things that must be done are intellectually taxing, indeed much sales technique is based on common sense, but it must be carefully orchestrated to create the best approach. Habits and reflexes must be built up and some aspects can only be refined through experience. It is certain that many consultants can make a good job of selling (some have become excellent and make many a salesperson elsewhere look to their laurels), provided the task is approached thoroughly, systematically and creatively.

The basis for the techniques involved is similar, regardless of method and must reflect not only the sales objectives but also the way clients buy consultancy services. In addition, everything we will now deal with can be used in contacts with:

- *Existing clients* (those already worked for and their colleagues in the same company)

- *Enquirers* (those who take the initiative and make the first contact requesting information, advice or discussion)

- *Intermediaries* (those who can recommend your services to others). Every area of consultancy will have categories of intermediary that are almost as important as clients. These may include those such as banks, or even other consultants

The word 'prospect' is used to indicate people who might have a need for your services, but are not yet clients. It is to the client's thinking that we now turn.

The basis for sales technique

The core of what makes the basis for sales technique is twofold, and both elements start on the client's side of the relationship. First, we must consider the way in which people buy. Much as anybody does when buying anything else, those buying consulting services investigate options and weigh up the pros and cons of any given case (and often, of course, they are intentionally checking out several options alongside each other).

How do they do this? They go through a particular sequence of thinking, one identified by psychologists way back and paraphrased here. They say to themselves:

• I am important and want to be respected

• Consider my needs

• Will your ideas help me?

• What are the facts?

• What are the snags?

• What shall I do?

• I approve/disapprove

Smart things
to say
Selling: is best viewed as
helping people
to buy

Each step in the process must be taken before the buyer will willingly move on to the next one. Some decisions can be taken at once while others require a pause between each stage.

In buying consultancy, decisions follow this seven-stage process, but execution of the process can be much more complex due to the nature of the client's business; the size of the organization; the people and functions involved; their needs; and the degree of influence they had on buying decisions. Selling is best viewed from this perspective. It is not something that you do *to* people, it is the mirror image of the buying process – something that is inherently two way.

Selling is a process of need satisfaction, and research shows two facts that are extremely valuable to sellers. Firstly, that interviews are much more successful when the client's needs are clearly identified. Secondly, as a result, they are less successful when their needs are only implied. Asking is thus as important as telling.

Nothing is successfully sold unless a client willingly buys. This is encouraged by offering satisfied needs as reasons for buying, i.e. perfect holes, not precision drills; reduced administrative costs, not computer programs. To follow the buying mind's seven-step process is vital in professional selling. There is a need to relate what is done in selling closely to the client's point of view; this can only be done if it is thought through carefully. Your sales approach must be, in a word: planned.

Planning for success

If you appear, indeed, are more attuned to the client's thinking than others, you will create a better, and easier, basis for everything you do.

So, *The first rule about preparing to sell is simple – you must do it.* Perhaps more business is lost because people believe that what needs to be done can be done 'off the top of the head' than for any other reason. Conversely, it seems apparent that successful salespeople, in any field in fact, are always those that do their homework.

Preparation may mean a moment's thought before your secretary shows a prospective client into your office; a few minutes with the file, notes, etc.; or a couple of hours (or more) sitting round the table with colleagues to thrash out the best approach.

Such preparation allows you to ensure that:

- The meeting focuses on the individual prospect.

- You are more fluent and confident in what you want to do and can save time (a valuable resource for both parties).

The process of planning is similar whether you plan to see an existing client, a new prospect or if a really major project is in view. It is an opportunity to:

- Do any necessary research (looking into the nature of the prospective organization and the person/people you will meet).

- Set clear objectives (what – exactly – you intend to achieve at the end of the meeting).

- Work out the shape of the meeting you want to run (not to prohibit flexibility, but to give you a main option and promote it).

- Identify the areas of questioning you will need to pursue (to identify needs; see later).

**Smart things
to say**

Planning sales meetings is,
quite simply,
essential

- Organize any support elements (what you need to have with you and/or show/discuss with them).

- Consider fall-back positions and different options (you cannot, even with good planning, expect everything to always go exactly as you wish).

You will always be able to perform better if you have thought things through; what is more your planning shows and people like it if you have taken trouble to relate to them properly.

Client strategy

Finally, in planning, there is the need to take a longer-term view, a 'client strategy' for those major clients, which in most firms produces a significant proportion of total fees and, hopefully, profit. Such clients, because of their complexity and power, are different in nature as well as size. They are not like all other clients, only bigger. This can rapidly be demonstrated by considering the effect of losing one. It is, therefore, vital that the relationship with them proceeds purposefully over a long period and this normally means planning at least a year ahead. Thus, the elements to be considered in developing a major client strategy of this sort include:

- Contacts in the client organization

- Other contacts (colleagues/associates)

- Assignment analysis last year, including any trends or opportunities identified

- Competitive activity, and relative strengths and weaknesses in terms of service, fees and terms, and 'presentation'

- Next year's objectives

- Overall strategy statement

- Detailed action plans

- Contacts to be made

- Objectives of calls – support required – timing and deadlines

Q: What kind of client mix, in terms of size, should I have?

A: The 80/20 rule suggests you will have 20% of your clients producing 80% of your revenue and profit. Current trends continue to indicate that major clients and the way they are managed will, in future, form an increasingly important part of many consultants' work. But you need to keep an eye on the proportion of your work they constitute, if it is too high then you are vulnerable – lose one and you are in trouble. Aim to manage and monitor the mix. To manage them well you need a broad appreciation of business; planning skill and systems; co-ordinating ability; financial techniques; and negotiating skills.

SMART
ANSWERS
TO TOUGH
QUESTIONS

Planning tends to be a weak area. Strengths can be maximized in face-to-face situations by thorough planning, so that the possibility of client rejection caused by unforeseen errors is reduced to a minimum. It is also clearly better to be aiming to create, at least to some extent, the client and work mix you want, rather than simply juggling to accommodate whatever comes up.

SMART VOICES

As a final plea not to forget or underestimate the necessity for planning and preparation, consider the following story about the nature of buyers:

It is any buyer's job to get the best possible deal for his company. That is what they are paid for, they are not actually on the salesmen's side, and will attempt to get the better of them in every way, especially on discounts.

This is well illustrated by the apocryphal story of the fairground strongman. During his act he took an orange, put it in the crook of his arm and bending his arm squeezed the juice out. He then challenged the audience offering £10 to anyone able to squeeze out another drop. After many had tried unsuccessfully, one apparently unlikely candidate came forward, he squeezed and squeezed and finally out came a couple more drops. The strongman was amazed, and, seeking to explain how this was possible, asked as he paid out the £10 what the man did for a living. '1 am a buyer with the Ford Motor Company', he replied.

Buyers are not really like this; they are worse.

If you sold to the motor trade you would recognize this instantly, but a serious point is made; when people wear their buying hat they are not on your side. They are concerned with their situation and needs, and they are getting more and more professional at going through a process which gets them, as they see it, what they want.

(Reproduced from *Marketing Stripped Bare* [Kogan Page])

Preparation in all its forms is often skimped, so while pressure of work (not least client pressure) may make it difficult, you will find it is a very worthwhile investment and an important, easy step towards positive differentiation to make sure you do it.

Clearly, with these basic tenets in mind we need to consider the dynamics of the face-to-face meeting, so we will turn to this next.

Face to face: the shape of a sales meeting

So, having thought about the process, and what we are going to do regarding a particular meeting, the next step is to run the meeting. And *run* the meeting is right. It is important to see it as something to direct, with yourself in the driving seat.

Q: I am uneasy about sales meetings, how should I regard them?

A: Resolve to get hold of the meeting, and ensure you are in the driving seat. Run the kind of meeting you want, and clients find that they like – and preferably like better than they do any competitors', and you will give yourself a head start.

SMART
ANSWERS
TO TOUGH
QUESTIONS

The simple procedure of, for example, suggesting an agenda can help you get hold of the meeting. An agenda that suits you, but that also makes sense to the client, and is certainly phrased that way, *'It might be most helpful to you, Mr Client, if we were to take . . . first, then . . .'*. This is an excellent example of what was mentioned earlier, sales technique coming over to the client as helpful and focusing on their needs. They are at liberty to amend your list, but you are likely to end up following broadly your suggestion.

Thereafter, the meeting will fall essentially into four parts:

• An opening, predominantly concerned with the identification and analysis of client needs.

• A 'presentation' of your response to those needs, offering solutions.

- Dealing with resistance (a less clear stage, since objections can come at any time).

- Obtaining willing commitment to proceed further.

What that final 'willing commitment' is to, or at least what it might be to, must be borne in mind from the start of the meeting. In some meetings the aim is to agree to do business; in others it is to agree to a next, firm, stage along the way – another meeting, the preparation of a proposal or whatever. In others it is just to obtain more information or an introduction to a decision-maker. Clearly, the more tangible a step forward is achieved the better, and having the ideal in mind throughout the meeting makes it more likely to occur.

Now, we will consider the four stages in turn.

Identifying and analysing client needs

Client attitudes vary at the beginning of interviews. They can be friendly, hostile, indifferent, interested, helpful or defensive. You may detect very particular attitudes. For example someone may be wary, conscious of dealing with an area in which they are not expert. Or they may be worried and see a risk ahead, something must be sorted out or they will be blamed – and to do it they have to put themselves in someone else's hands. The opening of an interview is therefore a crucial time for both parties.

Remember the first two steps in the buying process:

I am important and want to be respected; consider my needs.

These two steps make the consultant's objectives at the beginning of all interviews very clear:

- To make the client feel important in their eyes.

- To agree the client's stated needs.

Successful selling is particularly dependent on this stage in the buying process being well handled. Exploring, identifying and agreeing to the client's needs correctly makes them want to hear the proposition. Subsequently, making it attractive reduces the possibility of objections and thus obtains more voluntary commitment.

Often people will volunteer their needs and priorities – sometimes even doing so accurately! But surprisingly often they may have only a vague idea what is wrong (assuming a problem) or of what they want. This may be for all sorts of reasons: inexperience or not having thought it through. Sometimes too they may think they know what is needed but be basing their view on a misconception of some sort. Often, therefore, needs have to be explored, identified and spelt out before they can be agreed and priorities set.

It is not putting it too strongly to suggest that this is a 'sheep and goats' factor in selling. That is, those who find out more about client needs, really find out, and are seen to do so by the client, have a head start on everything else that follows. *It can be the first step to beating competition.*

So how do you go about it? Exploration can be carried out either by questions or statements, or by a combination of both questions and statements. Questions are initially safer and more productive, but they have to be carefully and correctly used.

The questioning technique most likely to bring results utilizes four basic types of question:

- Background questions – e.g. 'What's your unit cost per item?'

- Problem questions – e.g. 'Are unit costs a problem?'

- Implication questions – e.g. 'What effect are high unit costs having on the rest of the business?'

- Need questions – e.g. 'What would you like to happen as far as unit costs are concerned?'

Such questions are best used in sequence. Open or closed questions can be equally successful, but open questions (that cannot be answered with 'yes' or 'no') encourage the client to talk and produce more information. The type and combination of questions used is very important. Experience shows that asking fewer background questions but focusing them better, asking more problem questions, amplifying problems by asking implication questions and converting problems and implications into need questions works best and forms a logical sequence. By contrast, asking a relatively large number of background questions, fewer problem, implication or need questions, and introducing solutions after the stage of asking background questions works less well.

The reason for this difference in the success rate is very simple. The first follows the client's buying sequence, the latter makes you talk about yourself, your firm and your services – all of which distances you from the client.

Each type of question has an equivalent approach based on a statement, where the same sequence can be used as with questions, namely *background – problems – implications – needs*, and statements can be most confidently used when the consultant already has a thorough understanding of the client's situation. Thus, they are more often used after questioning or during subsequent meetings.

Clients with strongly felt needs will often buy with very little encouragement. Many clients, however, are satisfied with existing solutions. They will maintain the status quo unless something causes them to become dissatisfied. Consultants faced with this situation must, in fact, create some dissatisfaction before the client will consider a change. This must be done without criticizing the client's previous decisions, which may well create a defensive feeling. This can most readily be done by showing that due to factors outside their control, the situation is unsatisfactory. Many outside factors can be used in this way: other people's actions and attitudes; the behaviour of materials, products or systems; market forces and local, national or world-wide events; natural phenomena like the weather; and many others.

Clients will normally have a mix of needs and they will rarely be equally important. The next stage, as a client's needs are established, is to identify and agree their relative *priority*. Questions that will establish this must, therefore, be included in the early stages of conversation. This is important as clients have a habit of saying that something *must be . . .* and then listing things. Often there is a clash. They want something at the most economic price (don't we all?) and also want a rapid conclusion and result. Which is most important? Maybe getting things done earlier will also cost more – such things need sorting out.

This early stage is vital, since, as the old saying has it, 'You get only one chance to make a good first impression.' Not only are clients making judgements on competence and approach at this stage, but the success of all that follows is dependent on the information base being established.

What precisely is done next will be based on this information, and is the first step towards an approach that will differentiate you from your competitors and secure the business in competitive situations.

I understand you.

Actually your whole demeanour and conversation must say this. It is vital, no one is going to buy a solution from someone they think does not have a complete handle on the situation. This comes, in part, from asking questions, also from listening to the answers and making it clear that you have done so.

Offering solutions

Once needs are identified and priorities established, the next step is to show how satisfaction will come from the specific services or recommendations that you offer. Again, the action springs from the appropriate stage of the buying process. The client's mental demands are: *Will your ideas help me? What are the snags?*

This means that the consultant has four objectives: to make their ideas understandable, attractive and convincing, and to get feedback that the first three have been successfully achieved.

Each of these elements must be considered in turn and they then have to be deployed together in a cohesive and effective conversation.

Making ideas understandable

Three main factors affect this:

- *Structure and sequence.* What you present at a meeting should always be structured around the client's needs, thus *'So in choosing a system, your first concern is compatibility, your second is simplicity, and your third is productivity. Let's look at the compatibility aspect first, and then deal with the others . . .'*.

It is also important to conclude one aspect before moving to the next, to take matters in a logical order and, if necessary to spell out what the logic is – *'Let's look at the project chronologically.'*

- *Visual aids.* People understand and remember more when information is presented in visual form. Charts, diagrams, slides, pictures and brochures can all strengthen the clarity of the presentation. In using them, follow the basic rules: keep them hidden until they are needed, keep quiet while they are being examined (people cannot concentrate on two things at once) and remove them after use to avoid any distraction. Clients like it too if some of the material has clearly been produced uniquely for your meeting with *them*, if so, some things can incorporate the client's name or logo somewhere.

- *Jargon.* Every company and industry has its own language or jargon and your field of expertise is probably no exception. Some jargon can be useful, if pitched at the right level, implying mutual understanding. But overall the presentation must use the client's language. This means using words and terms that you are certain the client understands and avoiding words or terms which can be misinterpreted in any way, even simple ones – *'Our service is cheap.'*

In a technical business, the aspect of making things understood, clearly understood, can be easily overlooked (you may feel you need some help in making things more persuasive, but surely not simply in explaining your activity, services or a particular approach). Make sure you really do explain clearly. At least as many prospects are lost solely because they are confused as because they are inadequately convinced. Check if you are not sure. And remember that unexpected clarity when discussing something a client expects to be complicated will always please – it speaks volumes for your professionalism.

Making ideas attractive

This is the heartland of what makes your case persuasive. People buy things for what they will do (benefits, i.e. desirable results from the listener's point of view) not for what they are (features). Consultancy can do many different things for clients, but not all clients want the same things done. Thus, only those benefits that meet identified needs should be mentioned, and it is the process of selecting and matching items from the total list of benefits to an individual prospect's specific requirements that makes a particular idea, or solution, appear attractive.

Smart things to say

> Benefits: these are not what you sell or do – a project, a particular approach, whatever – rather they are what this does for the client. Talk about results and you will always be more persuasive.

There are normally three types of benefit which can be used:

• Benefits to the individual in their job

• Benefits to the person themselves

• Benefits to others in whom they are interested

The choice will depend on the needs and priorities; most often a mix works best.

This benefit-oriented basis of description in talking with clients is vital. It is another 'sheep and goats' factor. The most successful consultants do not sell simply their services – they sell benefits; that is what clients want to buy. But what, exactly, are benefits? This is worth a moment's careful consideration.

Benefits are what products or services *do* for the client. It is not important what they are, but what they do or mean for the client. To take an everyday example, a person does not buy an electrical drill because they want an electric drill, but because they want to be able to make holes. They buy holes, not a drill. They buy the drill for what it will do (make holes) and this in turn may only be important to them because they want to put up shelving as they need more storage space.

Consultancy is normally concerned with results – the situation at the end of a project rather than just the project itself. Even the simplest kind of thing works in this way – a client does not want a new brochure designed, they want to sell more (as a result of having an improved brochure).

Realizing this not only makes selling more effective, but also easier. You do not have to try to sell the same standard service to a lot of different people, but meet each person's needs with personal benefits. Benefits are what the services you sell can do for each individual client – the things they want them to do for them. Different clients buy the same service for different reasons. It is important, therefore, to

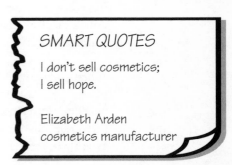

SMART QUOTES

I don't sell cosmetics; I sell hope.

Elizabeth Arden
cosmetics manufacturer

identify and use the particular benefits of interest to each. What a product 'is' is represented by its 'features'. What a product 'does' is described by its benefits.

The client is most unlikely to see things from the consultant's point of view. Everyone sees themselves as the most important person in the world. Therefore, to be successful, any consultant must be able to see things from the client's point of view, and demonstrate through their words and actions that they have done so. The chances of success are greater if you can understand the needs of the people you talk to and make them realize that you can fulfil those needs – and deliver the results they want.

Smart things to say

Empathy: the ability to put yourself in other peoples' shoes and see things from their point of view, and importantly (in selling) to be seen to be doing so.

This is essentially achieved by the correct use of benefits. In presenting any proposition to a client, even simply recommending a service in reply to a query, you should always translate what you are offering into what it will do. It is especially easy in technical areas to focus on features, adding more and more features as services are refined and improved. It is only a small step before everyone is busy trying to sell services on their features alone.

When competitive firms' services are almost identical in their performance – at least from a prospect's viewpoint, it can be difficult to sell benefits, since they all seem to offer the same benefits. Choice, then, often depends on the personal appeal of some secondary factor. But even then, there must be emphasis on the benefits derived from those features, rather than on the features themselves. Features are only important if they support the benefits that the customer is interested in.

Deciding to concentrate on describing benefits is only half the battle, however. They have to be the right benefits. In fact, benefits are only important to a client if they describe the satisfaction of his needs. Working out the needs, and then the benefits, means being 'in the client's shoes'. To know which benefits to put forward, you must understand the need. Firms often have more than one decision-maker, therefore it is essential to pinpoint your contact within the hierarchy in order to relate to them accurately. Sometimes different points need making to different people.

To do this it is useful to analyse services in terms of features and benefits. Thus an accountant might contrast:

- *Benefit* – provides a quicker, more certain audit analysis with less disruption of the accounts department, and results available for action sooner

- *Feature* – a computer-assisted audit.

SMART
ANSWERS
TO TOUGH
QUESTIONS

Q: How can I be sure I'm talking about benefits?

A: Analysing your services in advance will help. So too will two checks. Play it over in your mind. If what you say seems likely to prompt the response 'So what?', you are probably talking about a feature. If you follow what you are talking about by the words 'Which means that . . .' and there is no more to say, then you are talking benefits. If there is more to say, then you are talking about a feature and completing the thought 'Which means that . . .' will give voice to the benefit.

An analysis can be produced for each service or for a service range, and can be presented within a firm to help everyone learn which points are features and which are benefits. Note that not all the needs will be objective ones; most buyers also have subjective requirements bound up in their decisions. Even with technical services the final decisions can sometimes be heavily influenced by subjective factors, perhaps seemingly of minor significance, once people are content that all the objective needs have been met.

By matching benefits to individual client needs, you are more likely to make a sale, for the benefits of any service must match a buyer's needs. The features only give rise to the right benefits. By going through this process for particular services and for segments of your range, and matching the factors identified to client needs, a complete 'databank' of information from the client viewpoint can be assembled.

With the competition becoming increasingly similar, more buyers quickly conclude that their main needs can be met equally well by more than one firm. Other needs then become more important. If, for instance, a buyer needs tax or IT advice, he is likely to find a number of firms which all offer the service required, and all of which will cost practically the same.

The deciding factors may then become people, availability, service, specialist knowledge and so on. The consultant must therefore look at the 'features' contained by the firm as a whole and be ready to convert them into benefits to clients – in the same way as we can practise finding benefits for the full service range.

Q: What is it about my services that gives rise to benefits?

All aspects of the 'features', whether to do with the services themselves, or the manner in which they are provided by the firm or its staff, are sources of benefit to clients. Such factors include:

- Price/fee levels

- Availability of service or staff

- Credit

- Expertise

- Specialist knowledge

- Speed of action

- Training assistance

- Quality/objectivity of advice

- Time firms have been established

- Reputation, location, philosophy, size policies, financial and international standing

- The character, style and manner of you, and of any staff or associates.

Each item listed above, and more, could be a source of benefit to potential clients and help convert them into actual clients. By 'thinking benefits' and by seeing things from the clients' point of view, you can increase the contribution made to producing new business and increasing your firm's profitability.

Knowing how and why clients view your services as they do is a prerequisite to improving all the specific communication areas reviewed here and to making your own use of them become more effective.

Talking benefits is always a basic component of an effective sales approach; it translates the case into the client's terms, and makes it absolutely clear you are seeing things from the client's point of view.

Check you are doing it justice; all the briefing and much of the thinking about the firm and its services will be introspective, and may prompt an introspective view and approach, unless you do so.

Making ideas convincing

If benefits are claims for the service, such claims may have to be substantiated, as sales claims – about anything – are always viewed with some scepticism. This can be done by describing the features that produce them, or by reference to third parties.

Third-party references must be used only to support your case, and not as arguments in themselves. If a specific third party is named, it should be one respected by the listener, and should face similar conditions to those of the client. A third party should not just be mentioned, but also linked to a description of the particular benefits and need satisfactions that they obtained.

Thus, consider the statements:

- *'I conduct practical workshops to develop presentation skills in senior staff.'*
- *'I conduct . . . and have run such events for X and Y' [where X and Y are appropriately chosen firms].*
- *'I conduct . . . for X and Y. In the case of Y, we were able to incorporate rehearsals of actual planned client presentations, which they were convinced then went better as a result.'*

Each is progressively more powerful. If a specific example of business gained can be added to the third, so much the better.

Q: How else can you phrase things?

A: You need to create a fluent conversation rather than use these techniques mechanistically. Varying the way you use benefits and adding power – and credibility – in different ways helps the process. The following illustrates this, you can use:

A simple statement B – F

For example, 'You will get more assignments if you use Benefits that match the client's needs.'

A comparison statement B – F – WA – NE

For example, 'You will get more assignments if you use Benefits that match the client's Needs. Vague or unrelated Benefits have a low impact.'

Sandwich statements B – F – WA – NE – F – B

For example, 'You will get more assignments if you use Benefits that match the client's Needs. Vague or unrelated Benefits have a low impact; but by carefully selecting Benefits that have a strong appeal you will get more business and get it sooner.

(B, benefit; F, failure; WA, wrong action; NE, negative effect.)

The way you describe the firm, yourself and your experience are essentially credibility factors. Clients do not buy you because of a qualification or piece of experience; they buy your solution because such things help make it credible.

Obtaining feedback

To ensure that progress is being made towards your ultimate objective, accurate feedback is necessary all the time. It is then possible to be flexible and readjust as the conversation proceeds. By observation, by waiting and listening to the client's replies, and by asking for a comment, feedback can be assured, and monitoring questions like the following can constantly be answered:

- Am I discussing your needs?

- Is there any problem about how I am doing it?

- Is my proposition attractive, clear and convincing?

- Have I overlooked anything?

Such monitoring ensures that the client's needs are being satisfied, keeps the client involved in the discussion and prevents problems developing later on.

SMART
ANSWERS
TO TOUGH
QUESTIONS

Q: How do I keep all this organized, what are the key factors?

A: Presenting one's case is simple and successful if one follows these basic rules:

- Take one point at a time.
- Tell the client what it all means to them in terms of results.
- Show them what it is or means – talk benefits.
- Provide proof where necessary.
- Check progress by obtaining constant feedback.

Obtaining feedback, maintaining a two-way aspect to the conversation (yet maintaining control) is crucial. Some of it is as simple as making sure you listen. 'Pardon?' Listen, really listen and use, and be seen to use, the information you are given to tailor your case. Anything else will seem like the 'standard patter'. So the more you can link back, prefixing what you say by reference to their situation – *'Because you said timing is so important, I suggest . . .'* – the better.

Even so, with everything you put over carefully presented, there can still be certain problems.

Dealing with resistance

Instinctively considering possible disadvantages in contemplating a decision is a natural human reaction. In selling, such considerations pose resistance, though the tendency for this to occur can be reduced. Resistance is more frequent and stronger when needs are insufficiently explored, solutions are offered too soon, or benefits and features are presented too generally or if communication is simply poor and unclear.

Some objections are not inherent in clients, but can actually be created by the person doing the selling. Resistance has both an emotional and rational content. Emotionally, the client becomes defensive or aggressive, rationally, they need a logical answer; these two elements have to be tackled separately and sequentially if resistance is to be overcome. How? First by keeping your emotions under control, by listening, pausing and thinking, acknowledging his comment – a sort of 'sparring' technique designed to lower the temperature.

Next, rational answers must be provided. It helps to turn the objection into a question, to establish the client's need behind his resistance. Why are they asking this? Is it an excuse? Delaying tactics? Or perhaps they do have a point? An apparently straightforward comment such as *'It is very expensive'* may mean a wide range of different things from *'It is more than I expected'* to *'No'*, from *'It is more than I can agree to'* (though someone else might) to *'I want to negotiate'*, and so on.

Although investigating *'What are the snags?'* is an instinctive part of the buying process, by the time a client reaches this stage they may be sufficiently attracted by the proposal to pass on without raising objections. It pays to concentrate on resistance prevention rather than resistance cure. Agreement on stated needs, and careful selection and presentation of need-related benefits, reduces both the frequency and strength of resistance.

Some objections are simple misunderstandings, the real situation just needs explaining. Others are a challenge, especially those about price. Often such are best met head on, as the following illustrates. A management consultant, sitting down for a follow-up meeting with a client to discuss proposals recently submitted in writing, was immediately challenged on cost. 'Before we get into this at all,' he was told, 'you must understand that we have to get the best possible price for this project.'

In a considered fashion he closed the folder in front of him and responded to the effect that 'If it is the lowest price you want, we may as well not go on, as I know our proposals will not be the cheapest.' The client immediately changed tack, 'The proposals were very interesting', he did want to discuss things. The meeting proceeded on a rather different basis. This is less technique than sheer confidence. And selling needs that too, though it should always be based on experience and sound judgement.

You should rarely be caught out by objections you have not foreseen, at least in general terms. Thus, handling them effectively is another result of good preparation. There will always be some, however, that demand you are 'quick on your feet'. An apparently unexpected objection, well handled, can be impressive, and taken as a display of competence.

One more point here: always bear in mind the nature of consultancy when dealing with objections. Take price: it is, after all, a perennial objection. There can be a defensive reaction that is almost instinctive if price is challenged, and this can lead to adjustment and negotiation. But if you say *'Right, I suppose we could reduce stage three and save some money there'*, you had better be ready when the prospect asks how that is possible *'After all you just said this is the best way of achieving the result.'* Explanation is necessary, and a different method may lead to rather different results.

Obtaining commitment

Knowing that the objective of all selling is to obtain client commitment often obscures the need to remember how clients arrive at the point of commitment. Clients only willingly take buying decisions after they have investigated the options, weighed up the pros and cons, and are convinced that their needs will be satisfied by implementing a particular proposal. Thus, the best chance of success lies in doing a good job before the client reaches the stage of asking themselves *'What shall I do?'*

So welcome to the delightful world of closing. If you don't love it now, start falling in love, because that's where the money is.

Tom Hopkins, American consultant and author of *How to Master the Art of Selling* (Champion Press)

SMART QUOTES

Attempts to get commitment (closing) without first having made the proposal seem like the best way forward will normally be seen by the client as pressure tactics. The bigger the decision, the greater the pressure, and the stronger the client's resistance may be.

Closing does not cause orders, it merely converts a high level of interest into orders and low interest into refusals. Even when all is well, however, the client may not volunteer a positive commitment. Similarly, the client may want to make a commitment, but there are several variations of it, and the consultant wants one particular kind. It is in these situations that closing skills are valuable; such skills concentrate the buyer's mind on the advantages to be gained from the buying decision itself.

Smart things to say

Buying signal: a positive sign that the sales job is complete and you should move on to close and obtain a commitment.

There are certain behaviours, questions and comments indicating a general willingness to buy that can provide 'buying signals'. Tone of voice, posture, hesitation, nodding, questions on details, showing acceptance in principle, or comments expressing positive interest are all examples. These can be converted into closes, being careful not to oversell when the client wants to make a commitment.

The psychology of the sales process can be important here. Although this is the crunch point, closing can sometimes be avoided because of the unpleasant possibility of getting a 'no', but the commitment must actually be asked for: the only question is exactly how it is put. So, to put it simplistically – always ask for their commitment to proceed.

Q: Okay, I must ask for their agreement, but it can be embarrassing – how exactly do I put it?

A: There are various approaches. Here are some examples.

Direct request

For example, 'Shall we go ahead then and start getting these improvements in service levels?' This should be used in situations where the client likes to make his own decisions.

Command

For example, 'Install this new system in each regional office. It will give you the information you want much more quickly and help you to make more effective decisions.' This can be used where the client has difficulty in making a decision or has considerable respect for you.

Immediate gain

For example, 'You mentioned that this year the company really needs to improve productivity. If you can give me the go-ahead now, I can make sure that you see specific results within three months' time.' This could be used in a situation where, by acting fast, the client can get an important benefit, whereas delay might cause him severe problems.

Alternatives

For example, 'Both these approaches meet your criteria. Which one do you prefer to implement?' This could be used where you are happy to get a commitment on anyone of the possible alternatives.

'Best solution'

For example, 'You want a system that can cope with occasional off-peak demands, that is easy to operate by semi-skilled staff and is presented in a form that will encourage line managers to use it. The best fit with all these requirements is our system "X". When's the best time to install it?' This should be used when the client has a mix of needs, some of which can be better met by the competition, but which, when taken as a whole, are best met by your solution. Essentially it links the close to a brief summary of the reasons to agree.

SMART ANSWERS TO TOUGH QUESTIONS

Question or objection

For example, 'If we can make that revision, can you get the finance director to agree to proceed?' This should be used where you know you can answer the client's objection satisfactorily.

Assumption

For example, 'Fine. I've got all the information I need to meet your requirements. As soon as I get back to the office I'll prepare the necessary paperwork and you'll be able to start by the end of next week.'

Concession

Trade only a small concession to get agreement now or agree to proceed only on stage one.

A close should suit the client and the situation.

So far so good: the client's answer at this point may well be 'Yes'. But no matter how well a case is presented and questions handled during the sales process, the prospect will invariably have some objections to making a decision. Sometimes these objections are stated, but often they are reserved and come in the form, *'I'll think about it.'*

When this happens, simple closes may only irritate the prospect and the way forward may be unclear. Yet it is a key stage to get over, and the best way can be to list the objections:

'I agree you should think about it. However, it's probably your experience also that when someone says they want to think about it it's because they are still uncertain about some points. In order to help our thinking on these, let's note them down.'

Then ask questions to ascertain any final points of concern. Do not write any down until each is understood, and do not answer any points raised – yet. Flush them all out and be sure there are not more to come. Then you might consider using an additional closing technique: *'If I'm able to answer each of these points to your complete satisfaction, can we agree we're in business?'* This is the *conditional close.* Each point listed can then be answered in turn, crossed off the list, and the prospect's agreement with each checked, then the close is not repeated, but assumption is used to conclude matters: *'Fine, we're in business.'*

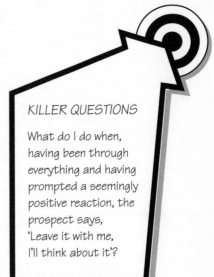

KILLER QUESTIONS

What do I do when, having been through everything and having prompted a seemingly positive reaction, the prospect says, 'Leave it with me, I'll think about it'?

This will not always work, of course, but trying may tease out other information. For example, if they explain the need to 'think about it' by saying that actually it must be cleared with someone else – then another route opens up. Who is this? Can you meet them? What is their perspective on the matter? If your contact is convinced, can you help them sell the proposal to their colleague?

If agreement is reached, then, having made a commitment, a client may need reassurance that they have done the right thing. Therefore, always thank them, confirm that they have made a wise decision, perhaps touch once more on what will come from it, conclude and leave promptly. There may be administrative points and confirmations to be dealt with, however, beyond that, especially at a first meeting, there are dangers in prolonging the meeting. Too many of us have been chatting happily at this stage when the client suddenly says *'I've been thinking . . .'* – apparently safe sales have been lost at this stage.

Good selling can often make formal closing unnecessary: 'Make people thirsty and you won't have to force them to drink' as the old saying has it.

Never avoid closing. Some of the business will go to those people most prepared to tie it down positively. It can be awkward actually to say *'Right, when do we start?'* (probably because you know they could say 'no'), but not asking – or saying *'Please think about it'* leaves you open to your more positive thinking competitors.

Of course, the commitment given may not be to do business, and the necessity for 'steps on the way' has been referred to previously. The next section looks, briefly, at the important question of follow up.

Follow up

If every new client sprang from one, self-contained meeting, the sales process would be much easier. But, as was explained earlier, it is not like that, as you will know only too well, one contact leads to another. A meeting, another meeting, a proposal, a telephone call; they follow each other and must maintain both the initiative and the interest.

Follow up must start immediately after the first contact, and many a job has been lost by default because of poor follow up. Accurate follow up is always necessary to correct misunderstandings, carry out promised actions and to show keenness for the client's business. After each call, building goodwill is important, making the client feel it was a worthwhile contact, even if his commitment was not made, that the time spent was a valuable investment in the future. Follow-up action should be automatic and made appropriately soon after each call, while ideas are fresh. A record of what was promised should be made as a prompt to the next action. It may take a conscious effort to make sure that the logistics of the business allow the follow-up action that is necessary; 'production' responsibilities have to be phased in with selling, and often demand priority.

There is not a great deal to be said about technique here, since it is much more a question of discipline and system. For example, make sure that you attempt to fix the next meeting, if appropriate, before you walk out of the current one.

Q: What do I do if things get 'stuck', I am waiting for a decision and get no answer or response to my calls?

A: Do not put off those, necessarily awkward, telephone calls, when the prospect needs prompting to tie down the next stage. Leave it, and the moment passes. It gets more difficult, not easier; and, in the end it may become impossible. If so, good prospects can die, by default, through neglect. So, be thick skinned and persistent. Keep in touch: phone, write, email and then do it again. Take responses at face value if someone says 'He's in a meeting', assume they are and ask when is a good time to call again. They will not make a decision to your time-scale, but to theirs. Make sure you – rather than a more persistent competitor – are still there asking (and demonstrating interest) when they do.

SMART
ANSWERS
TO TOUGH
QUESTIONS

Client development

Once you have a new client, once a project is under way, that does not mean the selling stops. Selling and doing must proceed in parallel so that the client potential can be developed. Here selling, networking and doing all overlap.

Make sure that:

- Contact continues and is ongoing.

- Vary the method of contact.

- Make sure everyone who influences decisions is kept in touch with.

- Make contacts interesting and 'issue led', that is do not just say '*Here I am*', rather give information, updates, offer advice and use this as a platform to sell (they will quickly resent endless contacts that do nothing but say '*Buy more*').

- Watch out for and record every potential opportunity for future business.

Maintaining the flow here is vital, good client development, and defining and implementing real strategy for major clients is not only an integral part of your overall marketing, it could just be the most important part. It is always easier and lower cost to sell more to people you know (and like you) than to find more new prospects.

Summary

There may seem a good deal to bear in mind here, and indeed there is. The logic of these approaches is sound – the most important single principle goes back to a definition used early in this chapter: selling is 'helping people to buy'. Viewed this way it is not an alien process, but an inherent part of your service. A considered approach, one that deploys well-chosen approaches and which also plays to your strengths

Mark McCormack

Mark McCormack (American sports consultant and author of *McCormack on Selling* [Century]) defines success in selling thus:

The qualities that I believe make a good salesman:

- Believe in your product
- Believe in yourself
- See a lot of people
- Pay attention to timing
- Listen to the customer – but realize that what they want is not necessarily what they are telling you
- Develop a sense of humor
- Knock on old doors
- Ask everyone to buy
- Follow up after the sale with the same aggressiveness you demonstrated before the sale
- Use common sense

I have no illusions that I'm breaking new ground with this list. These are essential, self-evident, universal qualities that all salespeople know in their heads – if not in their hearts.

as an expert in your field, will ensure a good rate of strike. Practice makes perfect. If selling is not your stock in trade you can become skilled at it if you view it as a conscious process. Success is partly in the overall approach and partly in the detail – but believing, or hoping, you can 'wing it' is simply not one of the options.

8

Writing Persuasive Proposals

At any stage of checking you out, the client has the right to say '*No*'. Everything you do – responding to an enquiry, holding an initial meeting and so on – has a cumulative effect. It is, when completed satisfactorily, a step further on towards obtaining a decision. Written proposals are very often a key part of the sequence of events. A good one takes things on down the sequence, while a bad one may stop progress dead in its tracks.

Actually it is worse than that. A proposal that is only inadequate in some detail compared to one from a competitor (and very often your proposal is in competition) may be placed second. Your proposal may be rated less impressive or appropriate by only a whisker – but you are still out. So the quality of written proposals is vital.

> SMART QUOTES
>
> Knowledge is useless unless you know how to communicate it in writing.
>
> David Ogilvy
> *The Unpublished David Ogilvy*

Proposals may vary. Some projects may be booked after sending a page or two of text by email (as was writing this book come to think of it – sorry I digress), others may need substantial documents as part of the process of confirming a project. Whatever is necessary it must be done right.

If putting things in writing is not your stock in trade to the same extent as other aspects of your communication, then it may be something you need to beef up. To be productive and successful you need the ability to decide what to say, to get words down in the right style and to do so quickly. You need to create powerful documents that inform, perhaps clarifying complex issues, that persuade – and that impress.

SMART
PEOPLE
TO HAVE
ON YOUR
SIDE

John Cleese (in his role as co-founder of training film production company Video Arts Ltd)

As a small digression I cannot resist referring to the Video Arts training film *The Proposal* (which I can certainly highly recommend).

The film shows a salesman struggling to complete a proposal. He daydreams of the rapturous reception with which the buyer will greet the arrival of his deathless prose and the certainty of an order to follow. But the voice-over interrupts – 'But it's not like that is it?' – and his vision changes to a less rosy image. This time when his secretary comes into the office to deliver the proposal, we see the buyer (John Cleese) sitting at his desk, a picture of hung-over misery. He is slowly dropping Alka-Seltzer tablets into a glass and wincing at the fizzing noise they make.

There can be few better images to have in mind when you sit down to write a proposal. If you aim to make your next one combat that sort of barrier, you will have to think carefully about it and invest it with some power.

First, let us define terms.

Quotations versus proposals

It may be worth being clear about what exactly is meant by the two words 'proposal' and 'quotation'. Although they are sometimes used in a way that appears similar, in sales terms they each imply something very different.

Proposals have to explain and justify what they suggest. They normally make recommendations, they certainly should assume that their job is to persuade. A quotation, on the other hand, is normally a much simpler document. They simply set out a particular – usually requested – option. They say that something is available and what it costs. They assume, rightly or wrongly, that the sales job is done and that persuasion is not necessary. This may be true, especially with repeat assignments. But many quotations should have more, sometimes much more, of the proposal about them. Here the review is concerned with the more complex proposals, though the principles concerned might also act to beef up any quotations you use.

Choice of format

There are two main overall approaches to the format of proposals. Sometimes a letter, albeit maybe a longish one, is entirely appropriate. Indeed, sometimes doing more than this can overstate a case and put the recipient off. It is seen as over-engineering. Alternatively what is necessary is much more like a report, though one with a persuasive bent.

Discussion document: a document for a stage before a proposal is appropriate, classically this sets the scene for a meeting, dealing with background and defining areas and ideas to be discussed at a meeting. Like all such documentation exactly how it is written is vital to its success. A subsequent proposal is thus an extension of this when both are involved.

Consider both in turn, and when and why each may be appropriate.

Letter proposals

This is simply what the name suggests. It starts with a first sheet set out like a letter, which begins '*Dear . . .* '. It may be several pages long, with a number of subheadings, but it is essentially less formal than a report-style proposal. This style is appropriate when:

- a more detailed proposal is not needed, because there would be insufficient content, or an over-formality;

- the objective (or request) is only to summarize discussions that have taken place;

- there are no outstanding issues (unsolved at prior meetings, for instance); and

- there is no threat of competition.

Where these, or some of them, do not apply another approach is necessary.

Formal proposal

This is a report-style document, usually bound in some way and thus more elaborate and formal. Such is appropriate when:

- recommendations are complex;

- what is being sold is high in cost (or, just as important, will be *seen* as being so);

- there is more than one 'client', a committee, a recommender and decision-maker acting together or some other combination of people who need to confer and will thus see exactly the same thing;

- (linked to the previous one) you have not met some of those who will be instrumental in making the decision; and

- you know you have competition and are being compared.

Q: How many copies of a proposal should I send?

A: The short answer is to ask and send however many are then requested. In many businesses it is common for there to be multiple decision-makers or influences. Where this is even suspected it is doubly wise to ask how many copies of a proposal will be required. If you have seen, say, two people and the answer is three copies, maybe there is someone else you need to be aware of and more questions (or even another meeting) become the 'order of the day' before you move on. One way or another you have to find out the role the new person plays and make sure that the proposal addresses them as well as others.

SMART
ANSWERS
TO TOUGH
QUESTIONS

In anything to do with selling, the client and their views rank high. What they want should rightly influence the kind of proposal you put in. Ask them questions such as:

- How formal should it be?

- What sort of detail is expected?

- How long should it be?

- How many people will see it? (As mentioned on the next page.)

- When do they want to receive it?

You do not have to follow their answers slavishly, but must make a considered judgement. For example, if you are dealing with someone you know, they may well suggest not being too formal. But, if you know you have competition and they are in discussion with other consultants, it may still pay to do something more formal than a letter; after all your document and someone else's will be compared alongside each other. In a comparison between a letter-style and more formal proposal, the former tends to look weaker, especially when related to value for money.

Timing

Timing is worth a particular word. It is naturally good to meet a client's deadlines, even if in some cases it means 'burning the midnight oil'. However, it is likely that people want your proposal to reflect your *considered* opinion. Promising this on a complex matter *'in 24 hours'* may simply not be credible. Too much speed in such a case can cast doubts on quality and originality. This is especially true of consultancy, and when solutions are positioned as being truly bespoke. In consequence, it may occasionally be politic to delay something, asking for more time than you actually need to enhance the feeling of tailoring and consideration when it arrives.

So, at this stage you know something about the client's needs, you know who is involved in the decision (i.e. those who will read whatever you write) and when the proposal is wanted. Remember the need for preparation: add in any time that composing such a document demands you spend with colleagues – in discussion, brainstorming, whatever – and set aside sufficient time to do a good writing job. Once the document is in the post, then – for good or ill – it must stand on its own feet.

Certainly once something has been sent, then you have live with it. You cannot reasonably telephone a correction later or send a 'revised page 7' to be slotted in by the prospective client. With all that in mind, let us now turn to see how the content should be arranged and dealt with in a proposal.

> **SMART QUOTES**
>
> What is written without effort is in general read without pleasure.
>
> Samuel Johnson

Proposal content and arrangement

While the form and certainly the content of a proposal can vary, the main divisions are best described as:

• The introduction (often preceded by a contents page)

• The statement of need

• The recommendations (or solution)

- Areas of detail (such as costs, timing, logistics, staffing and technical specification)

- Closing statement (or summary)

- Additional information (of prime or lesser importance – in the form of appendices)

Each section may need a number of subheadings. The length of these subheadings may vary with context but they form a convenient way of reviewing the key issues about the construction of a proposal and are thus commented on in turn:

Title/contents page

A proposal of any complexity needs the equivalent of a book's title page. This states who, or which organization, it is for, what it is about and who it is from. This page can also give the contact details of the proposer (which, if not here, certainly must be somewhere in the proposal) and some people like to feature the logo of the recipient organization on it, as well as their own.

This should be followed by a front sheet on which the contents of the proposal are listed and which gives the page numbers. It may make it look more interesting if there are subheadings as well as main headings, especially if the main headings have to be bland, for instance '*The Introduction*'.

Note: the headings that follow below are descriptive of the functions and role of the sections, not recommendations for headings you should necessarily use.

Introduction

Remember that a proposal is a sales document. The opening must command attention, establish interest and lead into the main text, making people want to read on. As the introduction has to undertake a number of important, yet routine, tasks, ahead of them it may be best to start with a sentence (or more) that is interesting, rings bells with the client and sets the tone for the document.

Thereafter there are a number of other roles for the introduction, for instance it may need to:

- Establish the background
- Refer to past meetings and discussions
- Recap decisions made to date
- Quote experience
- Acknowledge terms of reference
- List the names of those involved in the discussions and/or preparation of the document

As none of this is as interesting as what will follow (if it is, then you do have a problem!) this section should concentrate on essentials and be kept short. Its final words should act as a bridge to the next section.

Statement of need

This section needs to set out, with total clarity, the brief in terms of the needs of the client. It describes the scope of the requirement, and may well act to recap and confirm what was agreed at a prior meeting that the proposal would cover.

It is easy to ask why this section should be necessary. Surely the client knows what they want? Indeed, they have perhaps just spent a considerable amount of time telling you exactly that. But this statement is still important.

Its role is to make clear that *you do have complete understanding* of the situation. It emphasizes the identity of views between the two parties and gives credibility to your later suggestions by making clear that they are based firmly on the real – and individual – needs that exist. Without this it might be possible for the client to assume that you are suggesting what is best (or perhaps most profitable) for you; or simply making a standard suggestion.

This section is also of key importance if the proposal is to be seen by people who were not party to the original discussions; for them it may be the first clear statement of this picture. Again this part should link naturally into the next section.

Recommendation or solution

This may well be the longest section and needs to be logically arranged and divided (as do all the sections) to make it manageable. Clear and informative headings are needed. Here you state what approach you feel meets the requirements. This may be:

• Standard, in the sense that it is a list of, for example, recommended approaches which you have discussed and sell as a standard solution.

- 'Bespoke', as with the approach a consultant might set out to instigate a process of change, implement training or indeed almost any of the many things consultants do.

In either case this section needs to be set out in a way that is 'benefits-led', spelling out the advantages and making clear what the solution will mean to, or do for, the individual customer as well as specifying the technical features. Thus do not just list what you will do – put what the result will be or how a stage will move things forward once completed.

Remember, the sales job here is threefold: to explain, to do so persuasively and also to differentiate. Never forget, when putting together a proposal, that you may well be in competition and what you present will be compared, often closely, with the offerings of others. A focus on the client's needs is usually the best way to ensure the readers' attention; nothing must be said that does not have clear client relevance.

One further emphasis is particularly important here: individuality. It is so easy to store standard documents on disk these days, and indeed it may be possible to edit one proposal into a new version that does genuinely suit a similar need elsewhere (though double, double check that you have changed the client's name and any other individual references!). But if a proposal is intended to look tailored it must do just that and there must be no hint of it seeming standardized. This is sufficiently important to re-emphasize – bespoke proposals must *never* seem standard in any sense. A client may well know that you must get many similar requests, but will still appreciate clear signs that you have prepared something 'tailored just for them'.

Only when this section has been covered thoroughly should you move on to refer to costs, because only when the client appreciates exactly what value and benefits are being provided can they consider costs in context.

Costs

Fees and all costs must be stated clearly, and not look disguised (though certain techniques for presenting the figures are useful, for example amortizing costs – describing something as £1,000 per month, rather than £12,000 for the year; describing and costing stages separately – such as preparing and conducting training). Such factors were described in Chapter 3.

All the necessary detail must be there, including any items that are:

• Options

• Extras

• Associated expenses

These must be shown and made clear. Remember the client lost because of a misunderstanding over travel costs – see page 45).

Without returning to all the details of pricing policy, do note that:

• Price should be linked as closely as possible to benefits.

• This section must establish or reinforce that you offer value for money, not just state figures baldly.

• Invoicing details and trading terms often need including, and must always be clear; mistakes here tend to be expensive (in the UK remember to make clear whether the price is inclusive of VAT).

- Overseas, attention must be given to currency considerations.

- Comparisons may need to be made with competition or with past projects.

- Range figures (necessary in some kinds of consultancy) must be used carefully (do not make the gap too wide and never go over the upper range figure).

Look carefully at how you arrange this section; it is not just facts and numbers, it must be as persuasive as any other part of the document.

Q: Won't some people turn straight to the 'costs' section?

A: Yes, without a doubt this happens – indeed, it is only realistic to assume that some readers will look at this page or pages before reading **anything** else. Certainly for them there needs to be sufficient explanation, cost justification and, above all, clear benefits, linked in here. Just the bald figures can be very off-putting. This section must not only deal with its discrete topic, it must act to persuade the reader who start here that it is worth turning to the front and reading through from the beginning. Write it to achieve just that.

SMART
ANSWERS
TO TOUGH
QUESTIONS

Areas of detail

There are additional topics that it may be necessary to deal with here, as mentioned above: timing, logistics, staffing, etc. Sometimes these are best combined with costs within one section. Not if there are too many perhaps but, for example, costs and timing go well together, with perhaps one other separate, numbered, section dealing with any final topics before moving on.

John de Forte and Guy Jones

In *Proposals, Pitches and Beauty Parades* John de Forte and Guy Jones focus primarily on the most complex areas of proposing, those where competitive tendering is the best description of what occurs. Here the presentation of price is perhaps even more important, but their advice is good for any situation:

> Treat it [presenting the price] as an opportunity to convey positive messages about your commitment to giving value for money and how you intend to help the client monitor and control costs; try to show that you want the service to be as cost-effective as possible. . . . Apart from giving the fee itself, describe also the basis of charging and, if it is a long-term assignment, how fee levels might be determined in the future or when it would be appropriate to review them. If a detailed fee analysis is required, this may be better dealt with in an appendix.

The principles here are similar to those for handling costs. Matters such as timing must be made completely clear and all possibilities of misunderstanding or omission avoided.

Bear the need for individuality and a tailored approach in mind; for instance, a biographical note about yourself or colleagues needs to be tailored to any specific proposal.

Summary or closing statement

The final section must act to round off the document and it has a number of specific jobs to do. Its first, and perhaps most important, task is of course to summarize. All the threads must be drawn together and key aspects emphasized. A summary fulfils a number of purposes:

- It is a useful conclusion for all readers and should ensure the proposal ends on a note that they can easily agree is an effective summary. Because this is often the most difficult part of the document to write, it is also a part that can impress disproportionately. Readers know good summarizing is not easy and they respect the writer who achieves it. It is a clear sign of professional competence.

- It is useful too in influencing others around the decision-maker, who may study the summary but not go through the whole proposal in detail.

- It ensures the final word, and the final impression left with the reader, is about benefits and value for money.

Q: What about an 'executive summary', should I use that style?

A: An 'executive summary' is placed at the start of the document to do much the same job as one at the end. In part it is a matter of taste (or of what the client wants – ask), sometimes we can utilize both. The only other guide that seems useful is that a traditional summary (at the end) is best for the person involved in the proposal. They will read it through and this positioning provides the most logical explanation. For recommenders or others less involved, the executive summary may be preferred. Whichever is used it must be well written, and remember a short final word is necessary even when the main summary is placed early on.

SMART
ANSWERS
TO TOUGH
QUESTIONS

In addition, it can be useful to:

- Recap key points (as well as key benefits).

- Stress that the proposals are, in effect, the mutual conclusions of both parties (if this is so).

- Link to action, action dates and details of contact (though this could equally be dealt with in the covering letter).

- Invoke a sense of urgency (you will normally hope for things to be tied down promptly, but ultimately need to respect the prospect's timing).

Other matters

The key things here are *appendices.* It is important that proposals, like any document, flow. The argument they present must proceed logically and there must be no distractions from the developing picture. Periodically, there is sometimes a need to go into deep detail. Especially if this is technical, tedious or if it involves numerous figures – however necessary the content may be – it is better not to let such detail slow and interrupt the flow of the argument. Such information can usefully be referred to at the appropriate point, but with a note that the 'chapter and verse' of it appears in an appendix. Be specific, saying for example: 'This detail will be found in Appendix 2: *Costs and timing*, which appears on page 21'.

This arrangement can be used for a variety of elements: from terms and conditions to details inherent in the project (e.g. a computer systems project might list recommended hardware details at the end).

Next, assuming proposals arrive safely and are read, there is another possibility that their use may link to that needs some thought.

The presentation of proposals

Some proposals are posted just like a letter; once in front of the prospect they must do their work alone, though they may be followed up in numerous ways: by letter, telephone and so on (persistence here can pay dividends). Incidentally, consider carefully emailing proposals. This can be satisfactory, especially in sending something to people you know well (or if asked), but it does not put something as smart as a bound document on their desk. Speed may be of the essence sometimes, but you can always follow up an email with a copy sent physically.

Once received, sometimes you know that complex proposals, especially those involving more than one person in the decision, will be the subject of formal presentations. These can happen in two main ways:

- The proposal is sent, then a presentation is made later to those who have (or should have!) read the document.

- The presentation is made first, with the detailed proposal being left as a permanent reminder of the presentation's content.

If such an arrangement is made in advance, then the proposal needs to reflect what it is. For example, you may need more detail in a proposal that has to stand on its own than one that follows a presentation. It might sometimes be possible to (with the prospect's agreement) delay completing the proposal until after a presentation, thereby allowing the inclusion of any final elements stemming from any feedback arising during the presentation meeting. Alternatively you can issue a revised version at this stage, either amending or adding an appendix.

Certainly there should be a close parallel between the two entities so that it is clear how anything being said at a presentation relates to the proposal. Rarely should any of the proposal be read out verbatim. What is usually most important is for additional explanation, examples and exemplification of what has been written to be given verbally.

It may cause confusion if, say, a proposal with eight main headings is discussed at a meeting with nine or ten items being run through (certainly without explanation). It is helpful if you can organize so that the job of preparing the proposal and the presentation overlap and are kept close.

A final idea here may be useful: more than one company I know print out – for themselves – a 'presentation copy' of the proposal in a larger than normal format or type size. This enables it to be easily referred to by someone standing in presentation style at a meeting. It also gives additional space to annotate the document with any additional notes that will help to guide the presentation along precisely. Just remember that page numbers will be different on the different versions and do not let this cause confusion.

Two rules

These are obvious but still apt sometimes to be overlooked.

- Make sure every proposal *looks good*. Use plenty of headings, bold type where appropriate and set the thing out to look professional. Do not cramp it – if it is being passed round the client organization, room for annotation is useful

- Check it carefully – *very, very carefully*. I know one consulting firm that received back a photocopy of the title page of a proposal they had sent in an envelope without even a compliments slip. The name of the client's organization was incorrectly spelt; it was ringed in red and underneath was written *'No thank you!'*

Having reviewed what a proposal should be and the detail of its content, we turn to how best to actually get the words down on paper.

Drafting the words

It may seem easy. Call up a Word document and start typing. Better still, give some thought to what you want to say and then start typing. And take care what you say.

Now, fine you may say, so I must take care what I say; and I do. Certainly standards have changed and improved in recent years and consultants are more conscious of the fragility of what they do, recognizing that in any communication even the wrong

SMART QUOTES

If you are an enthusiast, it communicates. And nothing communicates so much as a lack of it.

Rowland Whitehead

choice of a few words may create misunderstanding or dilute their professional image. But one form of communications lags in this respect, and that is communications in writing. Somehow this is more difficult. People find themselves originating material that is at best pedestrian and at worst formulaic, banal or containing a surfeit of jargon, officespeak and gobbledegook. Why?

Most often it is lack of thought and care. Writing usually takes place with an eye on the clock. Some text may be drawn from standard material (that may date back years and may not have been good when it was originated). Others are adapted one from another; as I write this I have just received a proposal from a financial consultant that halfway through suddenly refers to me as Margaret! Oops, but I understand how easily it can happen. Or documents reflect the – bad – writing habits of a lifetime, habits that perhaps started because there was no real guidance available as to what was best. In sessions critiquing material on business writing courses, I find that the worst examples are rarely defended. No one says: 'I thought long and hard about that paragraph and I believe it is the best way to say it'; more likely they admit it is unclear or gives the wrong impression and readily seek a better turn of phrase. It is not that wrong decisions are being taken, more that thought and care is inadequate as writing takes place on 'automatic pilot'.

Making it right

Good writing – of a proposal (or a letter, a brochure, a press release or anything else for that matter) – starts with clear intentions. If you cannot say *why* you are writing, then it is unlikely that you will create something satisfactory. Writing must reflect clear intentions in four main areas:

- *The message.* What it is, how it can be made clear, what effect it should have on the reader, what restrictions or opportunities the form of writing reflects (has it some space restrictions, for instance if the client has specified the nature of proposal that they want)?

- *The nature of the message.* Must it inform, persuade, change attitudes or motivate; or all of these and more? Whatever the intention it – or they – must be firmly in mind as you write.

- *The reader.* What are their expectations, not only for the message itself but for the written form (will they expect it to be long or short, clear, descriptive, jargon-free, etc.)? If expectations reflect a meeting already held, and found useful, then they will expect your written word to continue the good impression.

SMART
ANSWERS
TO TOUGH
QUESTIONS

Q: What if there is more than one reader?

A: A proposal has to be addressed primarily towards one person. If it tries to do six different things at once it may well fail in them all. It may need to make clear the line it takes in this way, that said there is no harm is digressing (in the text, or perhaps into an appendix) and making it clear precisely who the digression is for. Something might start by saying 'For those needing more detail . . .', for instance. In this way you can actually succeed at talking to more than one person and make it seem well constructed and useful.

- *The image put across.* What impression should what you write give of you? Maybe you need to appear experienced, helpful, well organized – again the list is long and you can doubtless add more. The complexity here is clear. There are many factors to bear in mind and all demand an active approach; in other words it is not enough to *be* well organized, say, you have to *appear so*. And could it just be that your intention is to appear better organized than you actually are?

Improvement may come through developing new habits. For example, one common fault in proposal writing is that writing is introspective: every thought (or even every paragraph or sentence) in the text starting with the words 'We', 'I' or 'The firm', when concentration should better be on the client. Resolving to twitch every time you do this and trying to express the same thought starting with the word 'You' (or 'your') may help kick start a different, and more client-focused, style.

The written word is not transient, as is a meeting. What you write may well last, can be passed around a client's organization and can sometimes come back to haunt you long after it is written. Have a fresh look at some recent examples in your office. Ask how they would strike you. Be honest. Creating something that has real impact, and will stand out from what competitors do, can be a striking, low-cost way to improve marketing communications. Any effort it takes can pay dividends.

Letters to clients

Let us consider letters for a moment, in part to lead onto more about writing that applies generally. Letters are too easily regarded as routine, and can too often turn out to be formulaic, replete with galimatias and sesquipedalians (i.e. gibberish and long words). Yet writing them utilizes the same overall approaches as is necessary for more complex documents if you are to create good ones.

As was said earlier, the first essential is to have clear objectives; to know *why* in the fullest sense a letter is being written. The second priority is to have some real structure in mind (yes, even for short letters). This need be no more complicated than the classic beginning, middle and end. Thus we might look at a structure, here designed to encompass letters designed to be persuasive, as follows:

- *The beginning* should command attention, spark interest and lead people into the main text.

- *The middle* should hold and develop interest, talk benefits and link to the close.

- *The end* should act to actively prompt action.

One important piece of logic, which links structure and writing, may be useful to spell out. Start with the end. In a sales letter – and a covering letter designed to accompany a proposal is certainly a sales letter – it is often a 'close', something ultimately designed to prompt action in the reader. It is surely logical to decide what that action is first. For example, say you decide to try to get someone to agree to meet with you, then you must write a letter that is specifically designed to make that happen. You cannot write a more general letter, and then ask yourself *'How shall I finish this off?'*

Language and style

Anything you write, a letter or a proposal, should be easy to read. Try reading something to yourself (or even out loud to a colleague for something important) and see how it sounds and how it flows. Remember punctuation allows the reader to breathe. You should punctuate correctly, using colons and semi-colons appropriately for instance, but simplistically it is straightforward to recognize that if you run out of breath when reading something, then it needs *some sort* of punctuation mark. The most basic rules – short words, short sentences and short paragraphs – work well. A common fault in business writing is over-long sentences. And very short ones can be useful. See.

Similarly short paragraphs.

A mix of these things may be best to create a suitable flow. Certain aspects (and these are not exhaustive, but just examples) need particular care:

- *First sentences.* If I had a tenner for every sales enquiry response letter I have seen over the years that starts along the lines of *'Thank you very much for your enquiry, details about our xxxx are enclosed'* I could retire tomorrow. There has to be something more interesting to say – surely?

- *Last sentences.* Similarly, something like *'Assuring you of our best attention at all times'* just ahead of *'Yours sincerely'*, or other cliché conclusions are excruciating and can again surely be bettered.

- *Clarity.* Things that are expected to be complex yet are easily and fluently explained automatically impress, and it says something about the writer when this is the case. Anything left unclear will not always be checked by the reader, and may dilute overall meaning and look uncaring. What – exactly – does a phrase like 'personal service' mean? Done by people? So? Spell it out.

- *Much used, but inappropriate phrases.* For example a conference organizer recently sent me, and other speakers, a note that said '. . . *I am also enclosing a list of speakers' contact numbers for your perusal'*. Useful information, but in my view perusal is the wrong word. I might refer to it if necessary, but I am unlikely to 'read and study it in a careful and leisurely way' which is what peruse means. It also strikes a curiously old-fashioned note and this alone should rule it out

- *Useful words incorrectly used.* My personal twitch is the word unique. Nothing can be very unique, quite unique or any other sort of unique – unique means something is simply unlike anything else

- *Bland language.* Be careful to be suitably expressive. No consultancy service is 'quite', 'rather' or even 'very', good. Sales-orientated language needs to have the courage of its convictions, if something is excellent, practical or unique – say so, and explain, descriptively, why is this so.

Again care and attention to detail is necessary. Just one word or phrase rather than another may make a difference. If you are seeking to create impact, be descriptive or differentiate – and regularly you will – find words that do just that. You are not trying to follow a long-established style or reiterate old-fashioned convention, you are trying to communicate and to make what you say interesting.

Experiment. Sometimes you may find you look at what you have written and suck your teeth – *'I better not say it like that'* – because it seems too informal or is not somehow real 'business language'. Maybe sometimes you should not go back, edit and produce something safer, yet more bland. Trust your powers of description. Say it – and you may well find clients like it.

So, make sure every piece of text, whether in a proposal or elsewhere, really works for you. If you know you offer special service, unusual value for money, and better technical expertise or communications

Publisher Management Pocketbooks, having expressed interest in an idea for a book, then put the project on hold interminably. Every follow up I made failed to get through. Finally, I wrote and sent the following, positioning it centrally alone on a sheet of letterhead:

'**Struggling author**, patient, reliable, non-smoker seeks commissions on business topics. Novel formats preferred, but anything considered. Ideally 100 or so pages on the topic of sales excellence sounds good; maybe with some illustrations. Delivery of the right quantity of material – on time – guaranteed. Contact me at the above address/telephone number or let's arrange to meet on neutral ground carrying a copy of *Publishing News* and wearing a carnation.'

I remember that I nearly did not send this and wondered, for a moment, if it was entirely suitable. I was pleased I did – confirmation arrived on the following day. So some creativity can pay dividends. (You can see the result of this in *The Sales Excellence Pocketbook*).

along the way (or whatever else) – then do not rely on people reading between the lines to get the full message, spell it out to them loud and clear. Give them something they will *want* to read.

You must persuade yourself that writing is not a chore, but an opportunity to impress.

One more thing: proposals (and many letters) must, of course, be *persuasive*. Many of the principles set out in the previous chapter about face-to-face communication can be used here and will not be repeated. By way of summary on the matter, this chapter concludes with a reminder of some of the key points.

Writing to persuade

Simply saying what you want is not enough. If I sent you details of something, this book say, and said *read this, I want you to*, then you might well reject the thought out of hand – *shan't*. But if I say that reading it might just help get your next proposal accepted rather than rejected or ignored, then you are more likely to begin to take interest. This illustrates the first principle. Persuasive writing must offer the reader reasons for them to agree or act that reflect *their* point of view, not say only why *you* think they should do something. Such writing demands empathy (as does every aspect of consultancy) and must exhibit a style unlike any other. So, some do's and don'ts which add to and pick up again some of the points already made:

> SMART QUOTES
>
> Writing is easy, all you do is sit staring at a blank sheet of paper until the drops of blood form on your forehead.
>
> Gene Fowler

- *Avoid* the introspective tone mentioned earlier. Starting every sentence, paragraph or thought begins with the word 'I' – *I will . . . I can . . .* and worst of all *I want . . .* creates a 'catalogue' approach, a list of things from your own point of view, which becomes tedious and is not likely to prompt interest in the reader. Try rewriting any such sentiment starting it with the word 'You'. It will sound very different. Thus: *'I would like to give you . . .'* becomes something that begins *'Your organization will find . . .'*. If the latter continues by explaining *why* what is suggested will be found interesting and how it can be valuable, better still.

- *Avoid* circumspection. A persuasive document is no place for *I think . . ., I hope . . ., probably, maybe* or *perhaps*. You need to have the courage of your convictions. Ideas and suggestions, or any matter on which you seek agreement, must reflect your confidence in it. So phrases like *'This will give you . . .'* are better. Similarly, avoid bland description. Your idea is never just *very good.* A suggested project stage should never be stated as being *quite valuable.* Use words that add drama and certitude.

- *Stress* the benefits. This reflects some of the jargon of the sales world. Features are factual things – tangible or intangible – about something. This section is approximately 700 words long, occupies three pages and deals with persuasive writing: all these points are features. Whereas benefits are things that something does for or means to people. So the benefits of reading these pages are things like: giving you an introduction to the principles of persuasive writing, helping you avoid key mistakes that will dilute the persuasive effectiveness of your writing or increasing the chances of your next proposal being accepted. Benefits should predominate. There should be sufficient benefits to persuade, they should be well expressed and, if necessary, backed up by proof or evidence (i.e. something other than you saying so).

- *Make it* readable. This has already been said, but making something persuasive must not obscure the other virtues it must exhibit. Like anything else, you will need a clear beginning, middle and end. In context here the important thing is to allow your writing to project something of yourself. Make sure it is not formulaic as if out of a text-book. If you want to sound friendly, efficient, or professional – whatever – make sure such characteristics show.

Like most writing, if you need to write something that must be persuasive it needs some preparation. Think about what you want to say. Ask yourself why anyone should agree to your idea or proposal. List the reasons; all of them. Then organize these. What are the most important things? How does one link to another? Arrange a logical argument, say something at the beginning to command attention and get the reader reading, and write to maintain interest throughout. The progression of this approach is a powerful aid to writing right and writing fast.

SMART ANSWERS TO TOUGH QUESTIONS

Q: Doesn't elaborate preparation just make the whole thing take longer; after all I know my own area, is it really necessary?

A: The answer must be a firm 'Yes, it is necessary.' But, in my experience good preparation helps you write faster and means that less editing will be necessary; it in fact acts to shorten the overall job. So list the things you want to say and the points you need to make, put them in a logical order, fine-tune a bit with the overall length in mind and then write to the plan you have made. This separates the job of deciding what to write from that of how to write it. Maybe I am a simple soul, but I find that easier – and you want to have sufficient concentration on just how things are put over to make it memorable.

A powerful start that then tails way will persuade no one. Lead with the benefits. Let features follow to explain. These pages will *allow readers to experiment with a more persuasive style* (benefit), because it is *written reflecting proven, practical approaches* (feature).

So, next time you set out to make a case in writing perhaps you might think about considering checking . . . No! Sorry. Start again: next time you send off a proposal, make checking that it is not just well described, but *persuasively* described, a priority.

SMART QUOTES

The ability to write well is the most neglected skill in business life. We all intuitively know that we need to use words well to succeed in our work, yet we continue to regard writers as specialists on the fringes of life. My contention is that writers are thinkers. Good writers are good thinkers. What business does not need good thinking at its heart? If you improve the writing ability of your company, or at least its sensitivity to language, you will improve your company's performance.

John Simmons, *We, Me, Them and It* (Texere)

9

Styles of Working

Working as a consultant can be satisfying and rewarding, but no one, least of all me, is suggesting that it is never hard work. Consulting work in all its forms can be exacting; what is more, you need to bear in mind that you are being paid for your time. If your time is not employed on agreed projects for clients, then, however busy you may be, you are earning nothing. You need to keep the job of running your business and of client work in proportion and well coordinated; the dangers of the 'feast and famine syndrome' have already been mentioned.

Doing work/getting work

Your time is going to be split between doing the work (and earning fees for that time), finding work, and administrating both work and your own business processes. The way you work must be effective in all these areas, specifically the over-

KILLER QUESTIONS

How do I balance doing the work for clients and managing my own business?

riding intention is to maximize the time you spend earning fees, while doing so in a way that still allows the other things that need to be done to be done effectively. Client work is certainly the main thing, but it must not distract you from essentials necessary to the smooth running of your business; and vice versa.

SMART
ANSWERS
TO TOUGH
QUESTIONS

Q: How can I prevent results in a bad month from depressing me?

A: First, bear in mind exactly what it is you are counting. There may be a considerable difference between work done and work invoiced in a particular month, and a large project being agreed today may produce no income for several months. It is possible that one poor figure disguises a better overall situation. Second, if you are watching the real indicators do not worry, concentrate on the tasks. One simple thing I have found helpful, following the advice of another consultant, is to keep a quarterly record; I have had a few poor months over the years, but quarters have been much more consistent!

This is a balancing act that needs constant attention: take your eye off the ball and you are in trouble. So what helps?

One principle that will stand you in good stead here is to remember that your best source of new work is your existing and past clients (assuming they were well satisfied!). Keeping in touch need not take up much time or cost very much and is nearly always worthwhile. Remember too that it is more important for you to sell to them than it is for them to buy from you. The timing that dictates things will be their timing, and it may well be that, however good a job you did, they simply have no need of your sort of services for a while. Eventually, of course, you must rule a line and further contact becomes a waste of time. But do *not* do this too soon or without a good reason; I have repeatedly over the years had instances of as much as a three- or four-year gap between assignments and yet been glad to have continued to keep in touch when something significant eventually materializes. After all, what you want is sufficient work in November, say, it matters less when the process that produced it all began.

That said, you will need new clients too, so the process of finding work and doing work must always progress in parallel.

Promotional and sales methods have been reviewed already, in addition to what you do there are a number of things about how you do it that are worth mentioning, especially when you are working solo or on a small scale. For instance:

- *Take action sooner rather than later.* If you identify a new contact, for instance, do not put it to one side because you are busy – send something or make contact in whatever way seems best and do it *now*. Otherwise, you risk finding that the moment has passed. The sooner you do things the sooner they can produce a result.

- *Take action regularly.* Consider setting yourself some simple targets, writing a set number of letters, or mailing brochures, each day or week. After all, what you want is a steady incidence of new possibilities that you can manage to respond to effectively rather than a lot coming all together as might happen after a larger mailshot.

- *Watch your systems and follow up as planned.* Do not leave things too long (at worst it can seem like a lack of interest) and certainly try not to leave longer than is appropriate just because of what client work you have on the go. When you consider the right time to follow up, you are choosing the best moment – the one most likely to produce a positive response – not the most convenient for you.

- *Keep in touch.* People are doubtless as important to your chances of getting new work as actions, so do not neglect your networking and do it systematically.

- *Do not rely on the 'provisional'.* Clients can be fickle and they are more concerned about their situation than yours. If they ask you to hold some dates provisionally, that may be no problem at the time. Then something else is confirmed and needs some or all of the dates. What do you do? The danger is that you postpone confirming the second, and firm, project in the hope that if the first is booked you can then juggle with dates to fit both in. You then find that the first project is never confirmed and the second gets fed up waiting. You can lose both in this sort of trade off; so take care. Many consultants have a simple philosophy – if something is booked firm, then it takes priority.

- *Record what prompts successes.* It is easy to forget details, so always note how things came about and use the information this provides,

David H. Maister

For long a significant guru in the United States, David Maister, has become better known in Europe since the publication here of his book *Managing the Professional Firm* (Simon & Schuster). This is not directed only at consultants but at any firm that sells its expertise, so accountants and lawyers are included. It offers practical guidelines on the whole business of running a professional firm and, while it goes into some matters (e.g. operating a partnership) that are of little relevance to the solo operator, much that he has to say will be useful to any consultant. Worth a look.

especially over a period, to condition what you do next – concentrating on methods and actions that seem to work best

- *Create visibility.* Find and aim to utilize aspects of your work that create visibility. This may mean anything from speaking at a conference to writing a book. (You thought I did it just for the money? Not so!) If this aspect of work is possible, set some targets and keep up the proportion of visible activities that you undertake

Ideas, resolutions and practices such as those listed above are useful, but they should not be undertaken in a vacuum. You need to know what you are aiming at. Some calculations may be necessary – and useful – here.

Specifying the task

You may say that your target is to make 'as much money as possible'. Fine, we all do to some extent. But a clear target not only defines what you are aiming at, it helps specify the action you need to take in order to hit it. Work progressively through the following points:

- The fee revenue you want to generate.

- The average size of assignment (based on historical data or intelligent assumption if you are starting from scratch). The ratio between existing and new clients (again historic data is needed here – if you are just starting, then all your clients will be new ones).

- The proportion of submitted proposals that turn into fee-earning work (maybe you get half, or more or less, of everything your propose – or aim to do so).

- The proportion of enquiries that move on to request proposals (it is unlikely that everyone you talk to will formally request specific proposals).

- The number of contacts you need to make to prompt the desired number of enquiries.

The last category needs viewing in several different ways and these can be mixed and matched, as it were, to create what you want. A contact might be a recipient of a mailshot or someone you meet at a networking meeting, or a whole lot more besides.

Of one thing, however, you can be sure. There is a sequence of interdependent actions at work here. If there are insufficient contacts, or proposals or too low a conversion rate at any stage – then the total fees you invoice at the end of the process will be less than you want. This is as unavoidable as night following day. Knowing this should concentrate the mind and help ensure that you put in the time on those activities that make the progression of events you want to happen, actually happen.

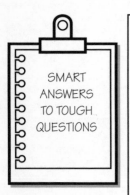

SMART
ANSWERS
TO TOUGH
QUESTIONS

Q: How many hours can I charge for in a year?

A: Perhaps not as many as you think. There are 365 days in a year. Allowing for weekends, public holidays, your holidays, a dose of 'flu and the day you just must attend that school concert, this quickly comes down to around 220 (do the sums and check it out). Then you need to estimate how many days other things – admin, selling, etc. – take up and also remove a few days that simply cannot be sold (Christmas Eve for one). You may now be down to 140–180, multiply by eight and you have your likely chargeable hours. All you need now is clients to pay for them. Seriously, it pays to target realistically and there is a relationship here between the hours you will work and the amount you charge.

It also makes a point about quality. If you dash off a proposal and hope it 'will do', you are simply likely to lose the job, fail to impress the client and reduce the likelihood of being asked to quote on a future occasion or getting referrals. If you are going for anything, give it your best shot, and if this occasionally means declining politely to quote – so be it. This will be respected more than something that clearly carries no conviction.

Monitoring progress

There is a danger with any small business that you think you can carry all the key issues in your head. Resist it. You need a simple system to monitor progress and let you see 'what you have on the go' at any particular time. This must be realistic. It should not include vague hopes of a project, or things you would simply *like* to do, rather it must focus on tangible chances of work.

SMART
ANSWERS
TO TOUGH
QUESTIONS

Q: I have two good proposals totalling £20,000 worth of work. I can't be certain, but I reckon I have a 50% chance of getting them both, so can I put down £20,000 as a likely outcome?

A: No. Be very careful. That is simply not how statistics like this work. On most proposals you either get the work or you do not. You do not get a part of a project (well, it can happen – but certainly not often). So you cannot make assumption of that sort.

Such a system is exemplified by that advocated by one consultant and described in the next *Smart Voices* box.

Consultant David Senton designed the work control system used for many years in one successful firm.

The system, apart from the obvious purpose of recording all relevant market information for future working with the client, had a number of important control and efficiency measurement functions. It provided all the information necessary to make decisions regarding:

- When to increase selling effort.
- Which market sectors were active and what changes may be evident.
- Whether price levels were adequate or excessive.
- The effectiveness of selling and the conversion rate from enquiry, through the various stages, to commencement of work.
- And, for the larger firm, it showed which members of staff were achieving their targets and even when recruitment (or the activation of sub-contraction possibilities) were likely to be needed.

The starting point was the Enquiry Form (see Figure 9.1) which captured all necessary information about prospects: client name, address and contact details, contact name(s) and positions, industry/product area, problem or work area identified and the action taken/promised – and allowed for a developing record of follow-up activity. This last could be used as a prompt – so that the last entry was always a note of what action was planned next and when it was scheduled to be taken.

The number of enquiries received, and 'in progress', provides a first indication of likely projects – and thus revenue – to come. Such a form is always completed and should specify the source of the enquiry (which could be external – from an article or advertisement, perhaps – or internal – follow-up action taken with a past client that leads them back to the 'what about this?' stage).

The next record is the Proposed Form. This is completed when specific suggestions are made to a prospect about possible work; this implies a suggested price, though this could be an estimate or range figure. This form also records: any additional contact information, what has been proposed (nature of work and value), likely timing, next action (who and when).

This is followed by a Booked/Refused Form. This again can update contact information, confirm the value, nature of task and timing. If work is refused, it should record the reason why. It is good practice to talk to every contact who refuses your proposals and discuss why they did not confirm – they will not always say, but progressively such feedback can teach you a great deal, and often the much quoted 'price' is not the full story.

Booked work can then be linked to a time-based system, what some call the Work Schedule, that splits the value of a booking across time, so much to be done in March, so much in April and so on: it is a diary of work to be done and charged for.

The totals here are a real aid to forecasting. For example, if conversion rates drop, maybe there is something lacking in your written proposals; if the number of enquiries drop, then, given the sequential nature of the process, more sales effort will be necessary or a 'famine' can be predicted somewhere down the line. The ongoing averages of such things as the time most often taken between a first meeting and booking work helps estimate the probable work load in future months.

It matters little how this information is recorded. It might be a simple form or it might link to a computer screen or a personal organizer. What is important is that any such system is well tailored to your business and the way it works, and that it is slavishly completed. Any lag or inaccuracies can put in jeopardy your whole basis for judging your order book and making future business decisions.

This sort of system is really not over-engineering and anyone should be content to take the time it takes to complete this amount of detail and work out and assess the cumulative detail. Being well organized allows you to concentrate on the key things that will generate your success.

SMART QUOTES

You can never afford to have any of the problems that you are solving for your clients!

Carole Edwards, Managing Director, The Business Skills Agency

ENQUIRY PROGRESS FORM

To:	
Ref No:	From:

Enquiry taken by:	Date:	Company:
		Address:
Source of enquiry:		
Stated need:		Tel. No:
		Contact name:
		Position:
Comments:		Nature of client:
		Additional information:
Action taken:		
Action promised (inc. timing)		

Subsequent progress:

Date	

Resulting fee	Value	Date
	Job Number	

Figure 9.1 Enquiry progress forms

BOOKED/REFUSED

Description of assignment:

Date:

Company name

_____

Value [____]

_____

Location [____]

_____

Ind. class [____]

_____

Work type [____]

Job no [____]

Refusal reasons:

Staged booking [____]

Price ☐ Reproposed ☐

Amount o/s

Other ref. nos. _____

Competition ☐ Age ☐

Client A/C [____]

Other _____

Engagement partner
(project manager)

PROPOSAL

Description of work:

Company name:

_____

Location	

_____

_____

_____

Value £

_____

_____

Ind. class [____] Group

_____

Work type [____]

_____

New client   Yes/No

ENQUIRY PROGRESS FORM

Source of enquiry ☐

Company: _____

Advertising ☐ Existing client ☐

Public relations ☐ Personal contact ☐

Address: _____

Centres of influence ☐ Seminars ☐

From: _____ via associates ☐

_____

Referral: ☐ From: _____

_____

From: _____

Tel. No:

Other: _____

Stated need: _____

Contact name:

Position:

_____

Industrial classification:

ACTION: BY WHOM _____

Comment:

BY WHEN _____

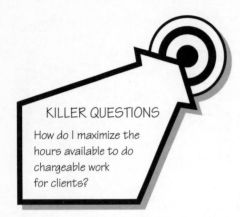

KILLER QUESTIONS

How do I maximize the
hours available to do
chargeable work
for clients?

Managing your time

Time management is a crucial skill for any consultant. It can enhance productivity, allow you to focus on priorities and ultimately acts directly to improve your effectiveness and profitability.

The inherent difficulties

So, if time management is so much common sense and so useful, why is not every consultant a time management expert? Sadly the bad news is that the answer is that time management is difficult (but there is good news to come). G. K. Chesterton once wrote that the reason Christianity was declining was 'not because it has been tried and found wanting, but because it has been found difficult and therefore not tried' – so too with time management. There is no magic formula and circumstances – and interruptions – often seem to conspire to prevent best intentions from working out. Some people, perhaps failing to achieve what they want, despair and give up. This is certainly not an option for anyone working as a consultant, especially on a solo basis; time is your most important resource – you either work to maximize the way you use it or suffer a continual drain on your effectiveness.

This is not an area in which you can allow perfection to be the enemy of the good. Few, if any of us, organize our time perfectly (even if, as I do, we conduct time management courses), but some people are manifestly better at it than others. Why? Simply it is that those who are more successful have a different attitude to the process. They see it as something to work at. They recognize that the details matter. They consider the time implications of everything and they work to get *as close to their ideal of time arrangement as they can*.

Little things do mount up. Saving five minutes may not sound like much use; however, do so every working day in the year (something over 200 days) and you save nearly two and a half days! Speaking personally I could certainly utilize an extra couple of days, no problem. If time can be saved across a range of tasks, and for most people it can, then the overall gain may well be significant. The best basis for making this happen, and the good news factor I promised was to come, is to make consideration of time and its management a habit.

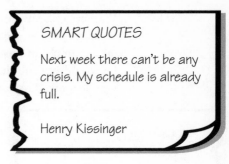

Now, habits are powerful. Ones than need changing may take some effort to shift, but once new ones are established, then they make the approaches they prompt at least semi-automatic. The process of getting to grips with managing your time effectively may well take a conscious effort, but by establishing good working habits it is one that gets easier as you go on.

The ubiquitous meeting

Perhaps nothing makes a better example of wasted time than that of business meetings. Which of us cannot remember a meeting that we emerged from recently saying 'What a waste of time!'? First there is the question of the time it takes most meetings to get underway. A meeting might be scheduled for 2.00 p.m., but people dribble in over the ensuing ten minutes, then a start is made, only to be interrupted five minutes later by a late arrival. There is a pause, a recap and the meeting begins again. We all know the feeling, I am sure.

Yet there is surely no reason for it to be like this. Some meetings can and do start on time. I can still remember an early boss of mine asking me join an important executive committee. I hastened to my first meeting, but could not find it. The scheduled conference room was locked and no one seemed to know where the meeting was being held. Meeting up with my boss later and explaining the problem, I remember he simply looked me straight in the eye and said, 'When did you arrive?' It was in the designated conference room – he had locked the door! I was never late for one of his meetings again, and, barring accidents, nor was anyone else. He not only believed it was important to start on time, he organized things accordingly.

This is a very good example of the effect of culture and habit within an organization combining to save people significant time. For the record, meetings need:

- A starting time

- A finishing time (so people can plan what they can do afterwards and when)

- A clear agenda (maybe with timing for different topics and certainly circulated in advance)

- Good chairmanships (to keep discussion on track)

- No distractions (to allow concentration – so organize refreshments beforehand and switch off telephones)

And, above all, meetings need clear objectives. Ban any meeting with a time in its title – *The Monthly Administration Review Meeting* – they will just become a routine. Never have a meeting *about* something: you can convene a meeting to explore ways of increasing fee-earning capacity by 5% in the last quarter of the year, but not one just to 'discuss productivity'. With clear intentions, good time-keeping and a firm hand on the tiller, as it were, most meetings can be productive. Remember, too, that the way you act regarding meetings is something your clients see. You do not want to be seen to waste their time and you do want them to be impressed.

SMART QUOTES

Don't call a meeting in your office: it scares people. Go and see them in their offices.

David Ogilvy
advertising guru

This attitude and approach can be taken in many areas. Respecting how things must be done if they are to be effective and organizing so that the best way of working becomes a habit for all concerned.

Plan the work and work the plan

The principles of good time management are not complex. Overall they can be summarized in three principles:

• List the tasks you have to perform

• Assign them priorities

• Do what the plan says

It is the last, and to some extent the second, that causes problems, so some other thoughts here may help. It may be useful to categorize tasks, putting everything that must be dealt with on the telephone, say, together. It is certainly useful to plan time for tasks as specifically as you schedule appointments. In conducting training on presentational skills I am regularly told by participants that there is never enough time to prepare. Yet this is a key task. Skimp the preparation, make a lacklustre presentation, and weeks of time and work may go down the drain. Putting the preparation time in the diary, setting aside a clear couple of hours or whatever it takes and sticking to that in a way that avoids interruptions must be worthwhile. Yes, this demands some discipline – more so if it is a team presentation and colleagues must clear time to be together – but it can be done, and it pays dividends.

It is a prime principle of time management that time must be invested in order to save time in the future. Sound preparation of the presentation may take two hours, but how long is involved in replacing a prospect if a client sales presentation goes wrong? No contest. And the same principle applies to systems; sorting something out so that it works well on a regular basis is also likely to be time well spent.

The last of the three main principles above is the one that needs most effort.

Staying 'on plan'

There are two main influences that combine to keep you from completing planned tasks. They are other people and events, and you. Let us start with you. You may, for example, put off things because you:

- Are unsure what to do

- Dislike the task

- Prefer another task (despite the clear priority)

- Fear the consequences

Or more, and time can be wasted in the reverse way. What tasks do you spend too long on (or resist delegating) because you *like* them? Be honest. Often this is a major cause of wasted time, as is flattering yourself that no one else can do something as well as you can. (Perhaps you do not delegate in case they prove *more able* than you at it! It is a thought worth pondering.) Such things may be one off or, worse in their potential for wasting time, regular. Certainly there are principles to be noted in this area: a main one is the fallacy that things get easier if left. Virtually always the reverse is true. Faced with sacking a member of staff to take a dramatic example, many people will constantly prevaricate. They may want to 'see how things go', 'check the end of month results' or some such, when swift action (all the checks in fact having been done) is best all round.

The second area of problems that keep you from key tasks is the classic interruption. We all have some contacts who, when they stick their heads round the door or telephone you and say, *'Have you got a minute?'* will take half an hour, minimum, of your time and do so unconstructively. Saying no is an inherent part of good time management. Telephones can also be the bane of our lives (though think carefully about how voicemail in all its forms can dilute client service at any stage of the relationship). But there are moments to be unavailable – some tasks can be completed in a quiet hour, yet take much longer if we are constantly interrupted. This applies especially to anything that requires some real thought or creativity.

A *major asset*

Good time management is a real asset to anyone's productivity and effectiveness. It is worth exploring the possibilities, instilling the right habits and avoiding any dilution of your firm intentions. As a consultant the prime balance that all this should be aimed at is that between fee earning time and other time. You need to examine your working practices very carefully, perhaps especially over administrative matters, to make sure you are not effectively working to reduce the fees you can charge simply because time is wasted.

SMART
PEOPLE
TO HAVE
ON YOUR
SIDE

Sophie Chalmers

For those who work from home, Sophie Chalmers is a worthy example and source of advice. Herself a recent regional winner in the Businesswoman of the Year awards, with her husband Andrew she started the magazine *Better Business*. This has become an important monthly read for those working from home. It offers advice on making the process successful and highlights the pitfalls (a recent article suggested that these include lack of motivation, blocked creativity, low concentration and more), suggesting ways to combat them. Available only on subscription (telephone: 0845 458 9485) it is a useful reference for many consultants working solo or on a small scale.

At the same time an effective way of working, and its attendant visible signs like reliably hitting deadlines, positively affect your image and, in turn, may influence the acceptance of your work and the strike rate you achieve in getting new assignments.

Getting the most out of the activity

There are certain activities that are inherent to the consulting process. Here I am thinking not so much of the way you, say, analyse a situation, though obviously the quality of your work dictates the reception you get and the likelihood of your being asked back after a project has finished. Rather, bear in mind that there are certain activities that, while being more a means to an end than an end in themselves, say a great deal about you.

If you recognize these, then you can bear them in mind and actively work to enhance the way that they affect clients and client attitudes. Three are especially worth a mention, and all are forms of communication:

- *Presentations* – the first one that a client sees might well be ahead of employing you, others are routinely necessary to present findings or recommendations. All need to impress.

- *Meetings* – these were mentioned earlier, and the way they are conducted often leaves something to be desired with people too often regarding them as, in part at least, a waste of time. Your skills of both participating in meetings and of chairing them need to be good. Clients need to find no fault with how meetings you convene and conduct go, indeed they need to find them surprisingly well planned, well organized, well prepared – practical and useful. Your meetings standing out from the norm is going to be noticed and, assuming it is for the right reasons, appreciated.

- *Documentation* – your proposals and reports must have clear objectives and be easy to read. No consultant can afford to be known for their gobbledegook and officespeak, you must ensure a fresh and effective style permeates your text and that when a document from you, even a brief letter, lands on a client's desk it engenders something more positive than a sigh of resignation.

Pressure of work can lead to such activities being undertaken largely on 'automatic pilot', a routine, serviceable job is done but nothing extra is achieved. It is always worth taking time – making time might be a better way of putting it – to ensure you are getting the most out of such activities. A great deal is hanging on these things. For instance, the style of a final report may directly influence understanding and the likelihood of recommendations being implemented; and it may also influence your profile. Every communication should enhance your standing and make ongoing work more likely.

Before moving on, consider the reverse side of this. If a document confuses, then it may cause a problem or prompt a query. You want neither. A poor phrase may be clarified in a moment on the telephone, but the client may still feel that there should be no need for them to do it. If they have to make such checks regularly, they will like it still less.

Client care

You will only succeed if you respect and look after your clients. Service is important in any area of business, perhaps most so when the 'product' is a service.

The basics apply. To use a well-known acronym, service must be PERFECT (see next page) though each aspect needs to be appropriately interpreted within a consulting context.

PERFECT service

P   *Polite*: this should go without saying, overdoing it can become unctuous, underdoing it can quickly be interpreted as rude.

E   *Efficient*: every aspect of the progressing and servicing of a client project must be efficiently handled, deadlines must be hit, promises honoured and things done in a way that suits the client with some real, and apparent, attention to detail.

R   *Respectful*: you do not need to go round touching your forelock, indeed you usually need to position yourself as an equal, but respect for a client's views, the culture within their organization and so on is important. But remember that saying *With great respect* when you go on to profoundly disagree with them is not the way to cultivate the right kind of relationship.

F   *Friendly*: in the sense of maintaining easy and friendly relations. You do not have to like all your clients to the extent of wanting them to come to dinner (nor do they have to like you in that sense). You do need to get on and be able to work together though, and just the right level of this needs identifying and cultivating.

E   Enthusiastic: without jumping up and down, you need to display interest in the client and their situation, indeed remember that lack of interest is a real turnoff. This needs to be coupled with a positive outlook and to reflect the fact that the client views their situation as unique. Nothing makes your view of the client seem wrong more easily than anything that suggests you see them as 'just another client' with everyday, common problems.

C   *Cheerful*: certainly in the sense that you ride above adversity. The times I have had to smile and say *That's fine* when faced with a client saying that they hope that some truly awful meeting room will be okay for a course . . . enough of my problems.

T   *Tactful*: you may be paid to say what you think and pull no punches, but that does not mean you do not have to think about how you put things. Putting sensitive issues, well, sensitively is good practice and part of good client care.

Hit the right style and degree of service, get to be relied on to deliver it consistently and, expertise apart, this can stand you in good stead. Sometimes the effect is very direct and specific: for example, get a reputation for hitting deadlines and you may be first in line for assignments with important or tight ones. Such may just represent work you would not have been asked to quote for or get involved with otherwise.

In addition:

- *Remember to say thank you* – when appropriate do not forget to say thank you and do so in an appropriate way. A thank-you letter is still appreciated (and email, though easier to execute, may not be regarded in quite the same the way).

- *Always hit deadlines* – and make sure that people notice that you have (despite the delays that the client may have put into the process).

- *Use agendas and minutes* – taking the initiative over such matters for meetings can seen as a courtesy, but it also helps put you in control and that too may be useful.

- *Document everything clients expect documented* – and anything they will find useful. Think ahead, asking yourself what they might find useful to have clear and in writing in some month's time.

It is worth keeping an eye open for any possibilities that might enhance the feeling of service between you and your clients. Just being available as a source of advice (you do not need to charge for every five-minute telephone call, do you?) is worthwhile; so too is sending information that might be helpful. For example, someone sent me an industry survey from the *Financial Times* the other day (one they knew I worked in regularly), whether I had seen it or not it is a nice thought.

A last thought here concerns measurement. It is one thing to believe you know how a client rates you, it is another to ask them. Face to face they may be more polite than accurate. So sometimes you may need something more formal. A 'client satisfaction assessment', usually a form that can quickly be completed (perhaps mostly by ticking appropriate boxes), can be very useful. There are primarily two main ways in which such a thing can be used:

- *At the end of a specific project.* This might be standard form or it can be tailored to the nature of the assignment (as are the forms often used after management courses).

- *At the end of a period (a year, say).* This would look at overall satisfaction perhaps involving a number of projects.

In both cases there is an overlap here with the actual conduct of assignment, but service is a key aspect. While there are various ways of doing this, a simple and often used one involves statements and a rating of agreement ('Strongly agree' through to 'Don't agree at all'). Service-orientated statements might include:

- Your communications are clear and free of jargon.

- Your progress reports are timely and useful.

- You hit your deadlines.

- You are good people to work with.

- Your interest in us goes beyond your brief.

Clients may well be used to this sort of thing in their dealings with larger firms, including the firm that conducts their audit and more, so it can be introduced in a low-key and natural way. The information is valuable and can help ensure you really are offering a level of service that is seen as appropriate (and as good or better than others).

SMART ANSWERS TO TOUGH QUESTIONS

Q: How many choices of rating work best on a satisfaction assessment form?

A: However many you use, make it an even number, there is then no middle point, it is not possible for someone to mark everything 'average' and the information they do give is likely to be more useful. So four or six makes good sense.

Summary

Working as a consultant can be very satisfying, but it puts you in an inherently exposed position. You are literally as good as your last assignment.

Not only in your technical area, but in your whole way of working you need to adopt practices that:

- Allow you to do a good job for the client.

- Maximize fee-earning time and minimize administrative time.

- Enhance your professional image.

- Make repeat work, and referrals, more likely.

- Minimize the time you spend on promotion and selling which, while essential, needs to be made cost and time effective.

Essentially this requires an active approach, just as was said, for instance, about time management. You need to develop the reflex and habit of thinking about what you are doing and maintain the flexibility to change as required to produce what you consider the best working practices and enhance your chances of being – and remaining – successful.

10

Career Options

Most people need some experience before they opt to become a consultant, so it is unlikely to be a first job. Although having said that, perhaps the exception is computers and 'new' technology where the experience seems to be able to be accumulated between the ages of eleven and twelve and sold on the open market as soon as the person moves into their teens! (I jest not, I have just had a formal invoice from my sixteen-year-old nephew – thank you Daniel, it is working well now.) Leaving that on one side, we look to the future and review certain aspects of how you manage a career in consultancy

Keeping up to date

One thing that should be accepted, organized and worked at from early on is that you need to keep your knowledge and skills up to date. This needs what is perhaps a more disciplined approach if you

KILLER QUESTIONS

Where am
I going?

work on your own and have none of the ongoing systems and processes that can drive development for you in a larger company.

The dangers of falling behind when you position yourself as an expert are obvious, so consider which of the following need action, and how much time, effort and cost are likely to be involved (costs for which you must budget):

- *Magazines.* What you need here will vary depending on your chosen area of work. Taking out a subscription may save money over individual purchases and the fact that something drops regularly and automatically through your letterbox may help instil the discipline of actually reading it (plan what you take for rail and air journeys).

- *Membership of trade or professional bodies* – and actually attending some of their meetings.

- *Networking.* An element of your network of contacts may exist specifically for reasons of advice, learning and update – this is best organized as a two-way street, if both parties are helped contacts are likely to be given more priority.

- *Courses and conferences.* These can be expensive, but attendance on some from time to time may be valuable, and they can also be useful as networking or prospecting activities (on the day before writing this I met some of my publishing clients at the London Book Fair, including the editor for this book).

- *Reading and learning.* This may need not to be the only book you ever read and there are a wealth of other ways to take in information at your desk, either through computer learning, use of the internet and many more.

- *Assignments and industries.* You may seek out particular kinds of assignment in part for the experience you will gain from them; certainly your work needs to be a prime factor in keeping you up to date (it is certainly the most cost effective method).

- *Joint working.* You may want to work in association with other consultants, not only to enhance the skills and experience that can be brought to bear on an assignment, but to learn from the colleague with whom you collaborate (this can apply to joint working with client staff).

There is a need to pace these activities as part of achieving an overall balance between fee-earning time and other activities. In addition, you may want to undertake activity linked to a formal CPD (continuing professional development) scheme of the sort run by the Institute of Management Consultants. Alternatively, a focus more specific to your area of work may be more appropriate; for example for someone working in my own area of marketing the Chartered Institute of Marketing scheme might be better.

Such a scheme contains its own prompt to your discipline, or lack of it, and as well as being useful in its own right for what it allows you to learn, it may give you added status that is useful in enhancing the profile you project.

However you plan things here, it should *not* be *ad hoc*. Do not only act reactively – *That looks like an interesting conference.* Ideally make a list

Q: Shouldn't some of the things I do be very specific to my area of work?

A: Certainly they should. As an example of how you can enhance the value of things in your own field, I would mention one thing relevant to my training work: training film previews. At such an event you can see a new film, assess whether it might be useful to you as an aid on courses you conduct, maybe learn something from it, have it act as a catalyst to other ideas for revised training technique and meet and network with people. Works well. Actively find such things that work for you and it will stand you in good stead.

of what needs to be done, perhaps listing knowledge and skill factors separately. Put priority ratings to things, set time aside as necessary and – baring emergencies – try to stop pressure of client work leading to terminal procrastination.

The time this necessitates goes with the territory as they say; skimping it can be dangerous, especially in the long term.

Ways of working

So, continuously developed, you will be fit for work now and in the future. How you set yourself up to work was mentioned early on in the book; here we look at the career implications of how you work.

Employment versus self-employment

If you need the stimulus of working closely with others or want support on one aspect of the business, maybe sales, that does not play to your strengths, then you may want to work with an established firm. In some fields it may be difficult to set up on your own without such a period of working and the experience gained is invaluable.

On the other hand in a firm the freedom to operate as you wish is less and, for those wanting to really do their own thing, there is no other way than setting up on your own. (Though maybe there are some middle ways, see below.)

Subcontraction and co-working

A compromise between the two options above is possible. A partnership may, if you wish, have partners working largely independently much of the time (while saving on matters such as centralized accounting). A great variety of differing associate relationships are possible, for example to:

- Facilitate co-working (together on one assignment)

- Extend service range (using the different skills of different people)

- Extend capacity short term (by sub-contracting)

- Make sales activity more productive (more than one person making approaches and having meetings)

- Learn from each other or spark creativity (two heads often being better than one)

There is certainly no one way of organizing matters here and a great variety of models exist and work well. Many consultants may change their method over time – in my own case moving from employee, latterly director, of a medium-sized consultancy to formal partnership to sole proprietor, but with a number of associate and subcontraction arrangements in place.

Building the business

You may start as a one-man-band and expand. Hiring staff and building the business is clearly an option just as in any other kind of business. The most important thing here is probably to be able to let go, to leave things to other people and hire managers to build the business alongside you rather than trying to control everything. Many have done it, others remain small or solo expressly to avoid some of the things that go with growing and running a bigger business. The job of managing a large consulting firm is beyond our brief here. But it certainly involves everything involved in running any other kind of business and the ability to do so in a service business, no doubt staffed by people all wanting in one way or another to have freedom to do what they enjoy most.

The work/life balance

The satisfaction of the work

You must be content with the consultant life. As was said earlier, it does not suit everyone. There are people who want more continuity, control or involvement and there is nothing wrong with that. But despite some potential negative areas there are few other ways to get as many new challenges or as much satisfaction.

Whatever the work, and the particular mixture of things you do, you must enjoy it (unless you are happy to regard it as 'just a job') and act to organize it so that such organization, in part at least, maximizes the satisfaction you do get from it. Recognize that this does not remove the necessity for hard work.

'The joy of consulting is that you are constantly learning about new sectors and new businesses, meeting new people and new challenges and generally always being stretched. This is also the pain of being a consultant because sometimes it would be nicer to just coast along.

Whether or not you take the credit, it is motivating to look at an organisation and realize that you created some really positive changes and results.'

Helping others achieve the results they want must be the greatest satisfaction a consultant can have.'

Kim Tasso, independent marketing consultant and journalist

The pressures of work

Let no one tell you that being a consultant is a soft option. It can be, and often is, hard work. Meeting client needs – and deadlines – travelling, preparing, actually doing the work, writing reports and doing whatever else your particular brand of consultancy involves needs (as has been said) good time management, careful organization and considerable willpower. The latter includes the confidence to say 'No' sometimes. Once on a training course with a consultancy company someone posed an example of the difficult and demanding client and asked how one copes with such impositions. I suggested saying 'No', an answer that was greeted with horror by the whole team. I extended the example adding a long list of further demands and deadlines, then asking if they would you agree to that. Everyone said 'No', feeling that the situation now described was ridiculous. Think about it. Such things are just a matter of degree and where you draw the line. If an extra meeting, travelling to another city (at a weekend perhaps) or other additional burdens are unacceptable (they may even jeopardize a previously agreed timetable to the inconvenience of the client), sometimes you need to say so. And ensure that your profile with the client makes doing so acceptable.

Consider the limits and aim to work accordingly. Of course there are emergencies and of course you can make exceptions and move heaven and earth to fit something in, but ultimately it is your life. It needs to be comfortable and you need to be fit to do a good job for your clients.

SMART VOICES

You have this huge illusion of control – you are the expert, the problem-solver, the coach, the guide, the leader. But then you realise you have worked every weekend for two months, know more about railway stations and airports than the transport authorities and your kids think they're orphans.

Kim Tasso, independent marketing consultant and journalist

Good organization – and effective pricing – can prevent you working ridiculous hours (well, most of the time) indeed a consulting workload can be varied, for example to allow you extra time to travel say during one year. It is also an activity that can be phased down towards the end of your career. If the thought of suddenly being retired is not something you want, then you can organize a period of gradually diminishing work at the appropriate time – though you will always need to allow some time to keep your skills sharp and your knowledge up to date.

Making it personal

However you work, one of the reasons for being a consultant is surely to work in an area in which you have a degree of control. This means that, to some extent at least, you can match your work to a variety of different goals. So, if you want to work in banking, business planning or Borneo (as I have done a couple of times), then you may be able to organize to make it so. Whether you can or not depends on:

- *The way you work.* If you are independent, then you are in control, but even in a larger consulting firm you can usually find a way to exert some influence over what you do. One of the reasons I moved from a medium-sized firm to working more independently was to be able to focus on certain areas of work. Previously these had been seen as something of a distraction (since I have been my own boss nothing I have elected to do has caused one single complaint!).

- *The market.* Whatever it is you want to do it must relate to a need and be saleable, and you must be able to sell it. Some things are ruled out by even a cursory look at reality: I am unlikely to find a client who will fly me to New York on Concorde, wine me and dine me on arrival and pay me a good rate as well just to pick my brains. If there is, get in touch now!

That said, there is, for most people, a real possibility of doing not just work that produces fees, but work that has other intrinsic attraction – if you work at it. You need a clear idea of what you see as particularly desirable, and to build seeking such projects into your plan. A balance is necessary. If you spend all your time hunting for special assignments, which may be more difficult, time consuming or expensive to sell successfully, then you may run short of overall work – and of money. More sensibly you need to move your efforts ahead on a number of fronts and ensure both that you create the right volume of work and that some of it is 'special' in whatever way that means to you.

Your preferences here may change over time, in light of developments in the market place or with your own situation. For example, overseas work may become less easy if a young family arrives.

At the same time you may want to pursue primarily logistical objectives. I like to keep travel – and the frustration and time wasting it entails –

under control. So work in London (an easy journey from home) is better than work in Manchester (which means a long journey) though if I have any readers in Manchester of course I *will* do it on occasion! Local work is attractive too. My prospecting and promotional activity must aim to produce the mix I want while keeping an eye on the practicalities, and the productivity and profitability issues as well.

Making it fun

It is worth a word to take the comments made above just a bit further. Anything that the work reasonably includes can be made a personal priority. Want to visit New Zealand, speak to a conference of thousands, run a course at (or for the staff of) an exceptional resort hotel or write a book? – then why not? The same goes for working in a particular industry or with specific types of people – or indeed for much else.

Such things can be momentary, a one-off but an exciting experience. Or they can be a new direction, one that leads to a permanent change in the mix of your work. Some caveats here should be noted. Be careful not to become distracted, spending too much time chasing some personal goal and neglecting to ensure the core business is as it should be. Similarly, if you start to move in a particular direction make sure that it is soundly based in business terms as well as just 'something you would find fun'.

You also have the option of organizing yourself so that your core business is successful and profitable *and* allows you time to fit in something completely different along the way. This might be anything from charity work to acquiring a new, perhaps non-business, skill or just having a regular afternoon on the golf-course or boat.

Active career management

Where you get to is influenced by many things (including where you start), other people and even good luck – though never overrate the likelihood of getting the luck. Circumstances, other people – including clients in this field – may assist the process, but there is only one major influence on which you can rely and which contributes more than anything else – you. As a consultant your career path and your business may be synonymous. Be that the case or not, you need to:

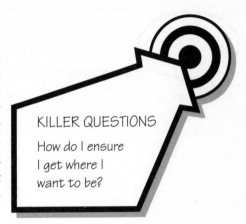

KILLER QUESTIONS

How do I ensure I get where I want to be?

- Think about where you want to go.

- Devise plans to get there (and take advantage of opportunities along the way).

- Actively take an initiative in this regard working in parallel with the work you do.

Career management: the active planning and implementation of strategy and action likely to assist in furthering your career.

Smart things to say

Like any other, a career in consultancy is what you make it. In any case, nothing so dependent on the personal touch is likely to *just happen*. Your must be your own catalyst to change and development; and remember that nothing is worse that pausing occasionally to analyse what you are doing and finding your strongest thoughts start with the words – *If only.*

Success is not a destination, it is a journey (this may be a cliché, but that does not mean it is not worth bearing in mind).

Afterword

So, how to end? Certainly a book like this cannot hope to be comprehensive, but it is intended to be practical, explanatory and unashamedly enthusiastic. Let me start with the last of these.

If consultancy suits you (and this book may have helped you to decide), then it can provide a worthwhile, enjoyable and rewarding career. For myself I got into it comparatively early (I was aged twenty-seven) and have never been inclined to seek a way out of it. It is, however, an occupation in which you are somewhat exposed. This comes through the work itself: you have to be prepared to trust your judgement and say what you think. It is also highlighted by the business process involved and, however much you can excel technically through the work, you should not contemplate becoming a consultant unless you are happy that you can manage both the business, the work and the process of obtaining that work. But again if it suits, the responsibility and the rewards are yours. I repeat: I find it difficult to imagine a better way of earning my living.

To help encapsulate views about being a consultant, here is the view of one successful independent consultant Gary Lim (who works throughout South East Asia and is based in Singapore). His comments range across the whole content of this book:

'Consultants should be able to see and measure how their work adds value to their clients. A measurement is how their work will help a client to reduce cost, increase revenue or increase profitability. This amount must be much more than the cost and trouble of dealing with the consultant to do the work.

Over the years, I have observed many consultants and trainers in different areas of expertise. The successful ones generally follow certain principles. One is that they focus on their niche. They make themselves specialists in their areas so that people will remember them when they think of that expertise. Being the best or very good is not enough. The consultants need to promote their expertise telling prospective customers how to contact them when needed. One critical characteristic is persistence. Many consultants fail to follow up on their leads or lack perseverance.

Consultants should have a clear idea of the profiles of their clients and know where to find them. In addition to clients, one needs to bear in mind the influencers. Of course, efforts should be made on current clients and their referrals. One important recourse for prospecting is the internet. I have it very useful to search for contacts.

The greatest satisfaction for consultants is when clients are completely happy with the work done. However, one caveat here is to be able to manage the expectations of the clients such that the consultant is able to deliver the results that meet those expectations. The greatest drawbacks can be the long hours and the need for a lot of stamina.

Getting the approval becomes easiest when a consultant is able successfully to show clients the value of his proposal. Carefully select those clients who are able to benefit from your expertise and willing to invest in your expertise. In my years as a consultant, I seldom have to bargain, though bargaining is a common practice here.'

Many of the processes that are necessary in setting up and running a business as a successful consultant have been reviewed here. It needs:

- A careful approach – doing the right things in the right way and concentrating on the priorities.

- A systematic approach – implemented with an eye not only on priorities, but on timing and co-ordination.

- A balanced approach – not least the balance between doing the work and obtaining the work.

- A client-orientated approach – because you are not the final arbiter of what works, your clients are.

Experience, as with any line of work, is vital. Things that originally seemed daunting become routine when you have tried and refined them. But experience must not allow you to settle into a rut, a way of working that becomes solely routine. This is a dynamic business. What works works – today. What may be effective tomorrow may need to be different.

When it does work, when you can look back at a project confirmed and the chain of events that led up to it and say – *I really made that happen*; when you can look back at an assignment well done, and at a satisfied client who may well want you to do more in the future, then you will reap considerable satisfaction.

Similarly, if in due course you look back and say *I'm glad I did what that book recommended* over this or that because it helped, then I will take some satisfaction from feeling that sharing some of my experience has been useful.

Go for it; and I wish you well with it.

Humorist and writer Barry Cryer describing his work (in his autobiography *You Won't Believe This But . . .*)

A man once said to me 'What would be your ideal day?'

I said, 'Arriving at work with some people, having a cup of tea and a gossip, taking them to the bar at lunch-time, doing a bit of work in the afternoon, more tea and then further merriment in the evening. That's my ideal day.'

'I thought that's what you did anyway' he said.

Consultancy may not be – cannot be? – so leisurely, but it certainly involves working with people and for most that is one of its greatest satisfactions.

References

The following may be useful to take matters further:

Professional bodies

First, the body that caters for the individual consultant, including those working freelance.

> The Institute of Management Consultants
> 3rd Floor
> 17–18 Hayward's Place
> London EC1R 0EO
> Telephone: 020 7566 5220
> www.imc.co.uk

Their journal is *Professional Consultancy*.

Secondly, the body representing the largest consultancy firms:

The Management Consultancies Association
11 West Halkin Street
London SW1X 8JL
Telephone: 020 7235 3897
www.mca.org.uk

Their journal is *Spectra*.

There are similar bodies overseas. In addition there are a host of specialist bodies where consultants are at least part of their membership such as the Institute of Public Relations Consultants and the Market Research Society.

Books

The two main works about the business of consultancy are:

Management Consultancy – A Handbook for Best Practice, edited by Philip Sadler, published by Kogan Page in association with MCA and IMC.

The International Guide to Management Consultancy – The Evolution, Practice and Structure of Management Consultancy World-wide, edited by Barry Curnow and Jonathan Reuvid, also published by Kogan Page.

Beyond that, there are a plethora of how-to books for aspiring consultants (like this one), typical is *High Income Consulting*, Tom Lambert (Nicholas Brealey Publishing).

Magazines

Here the following is certainly recommended for those wanting guidance on running their business (rather than on how to consult). It is my favourite (I write for it regularly) and is essentially how-to in style:

> *Better Business*
> Cribau Mill
> Llanvair
> Chepstow NP6 6LN
> Telephone: 0845 458 9485
> Email: info@better-business.co.uk

Index